Surviving the Death
of a Child

To Marlys
January 11, 1961–May 10, 1979

Turn around, turn around,
think of all the good times that we've had.
Turn around just once more,
think of all the good times, not the bad.
There's always time for living
but I guess this means good-bye.
I know it's very hard to do
but I guess I'll have to try.
I've seen you for the last time,
but I won't see you again.
I loved you as my sister
and I loved you as my friend.
I hope they find the person
that committed such a crime.
He took your life away from you.
He'll serve a lot of time.
Life is too important
to be taken in a day.
We tried to bring you back to us
in each and every way.
I know that you're in heaven
and there's something you should know:
That even though you had to die
I didn't want to let you go.

Lynn
May 10, 1979

CONTENTS

PREFACE

We are survivors, and we want to share a message of hope with those who read this book. Marlys, Fran's daughter, was murdered in 1979, and the murder is still unsolved. That single moment in history, when Marlys was attacked, not only ended her life but radically changed the lives of many other people. Since that fateful day Fran has been striving to survive, facing and overcoming the horror and despair of knowing that Marlys was taken from her. I have been her constant companion on the journey to healing, a long and truly never-ending journey, but one based on the knowledge that if we can't have our child back, we can, at least, be healed.

Along the way Fran and I have come to understand that while we never are the same person after our child dies, and in that sense we never recover, we can be healed. Our child would want us to be healed. As part of the healing process we have made some mistakes; we admit the ones we recognize. And we have made some good decisions. We moved away from Minnesota because the pain and the memories were so fresh and vivid there was no peace. That was a mistake, because efforts to solve the crime were slowed by our absence. But it was also a good decision, because we were energized and comforted by people and organizations, commitments, and events that wouldn't have been available to us back in Minnesota.

Surviving the Death of a Child describes one mother's struggle to survive the grief that every bereaved parent endures. It is a story of her faith in God and her faith in God's comfort during this most difficult time in life. And it is a story of love. Love exists in the midst of grief, and finding that love is the key to healing. Healing takes place only when we reach out in love; love for others, placing others ahead of ourselves, brings healing. We hope this book will answer questions that all bereaved parents ask themselves and others. But this book is also intended to bring comfort and understanding to those who don't know the pain of bereavement.

Perhaps the best part of surviving the murder, for Fran and me and others in our family, is that Marlys lives on in our memories. Many years after the murder, we know now that we won't forget her. We know we have given her the one gift she would ask for: that her mom be healed. Healing and remembering are brought together through a reality in which hope and faith and love come together in the struggle to survive: hope for healing, faith in God, love for others, that they too may be healed. Marlys would have wanted that for her mother. Her mother, like all parents who are bereaved, wants that for all the world.

We have met many bereaved persons over these years of healing. We hope this book will answer questions that every bereaved parent has had. We also hope it will bring comfort and understanding to those who don't know the pain of bereavement.

INTRODUCTION

It happens. Someone you love dies. Someone close dies. A child dies. Your child. You may have known it was going to happen, after a long terminal illness perhaps, or it may happen suddenly, without warning, as it did to us.

When you hear of someone's child dying, you close your mind to the horror because you never expect it to happen to you. But it does. There must be a mistake, you think. Not your child. Not dead. No. No!

At approximately 2:40 P.M. on Tuesday, May 8, 1979, Marlys Ann Wohlenhaus was brutally attacked, at home, with a blunt instrument. Fran, her mother, found her less than an hour later, lying in a pool of blood. No one ever expected it to happen.

At the time of her murder, Marlys was eighteen years old and a senior at Stillwater High School, in Stillwater, Minnesota.

On Saturday, May 12, she was buried from a little white church on a hill in Afton, Minnesota. The church cemetery looks down on the St. Croix River as it forms the border between Minnesota and neighboring Wisconsin. Marlys had been confirmed there and had attended regularly.

The next day was Mother's Day.

For those who mourn the death of a child, grief cannot be pushed aside or avoided. It must be met head-on. A parent's grief is so real it defies understanding. But it must be understood. Parents expect their children to survive them, and that expectation is so strong that they, above all, should look to God for answers.

This book is the story of Fran's grief and the healing path through faith that she has traveled. It is the story of how a mother lived through the unimaginable experience of finding her daughter, dying, in the safety of her own home. It is the story of a mother who has lived with what experts say is the most difficult kind of pain. It is a story of Christian response to a child's death. And it is the story of the torturous path that leads to healing.

Some days after the murder, when the rest of the world had gone back to normal, Fran cried out, in a moment of anguish over Marlys's murder, "I wasn't ready to let her go!"

No one is ever ready to let a child go. But even when expected, the shock of a child's death, so complete and final, subjects the parents to grief that is unlike any other experience in life.

Far too many parents know this grief. Those who truly know the pain that brings forth the cry "I wasn't ready to let her go!" will reach out to fellow sufferers to offer something to hold on to. This book is the story of those who experience a loss they never expected. It is also the result of my efforts to understand that grief, as someone who was not Marlys's parent but whose life was also forever changed by her death. It is a book for the bereaved parent and other family members, and it is a book for those who would comfort those who mourn.

In these chapters I will share with you what we call a "theology of accompaniment." I will try to explain how faith works in the lives of bereaved parents to bring hope of healing. Healing does come, in accompaniment by and with others who also suffer. As the bereaved parent knows only too well, being there is the only hope for recovery.

As with most explanations of God's action in our lives, everything begins with the story. So this theology begins with what happened. It is essential that the story be told and that parents be able to say to those who will listen that their child has died. Everything begins here. What happened? How did it happen? Why did it happen?

Marlys died from a violent and vicious attack, and those details have to be described. If she had been killed in an auto accident or had been the victim of cancer, that would have been part of this book. For the parent whose child dies, everything is part of the story that must be told.

In the telling and retelling, sometimes one finds that God has been present too. But first it is necessary to tell the story.

On that horrible day, Fran found Marlys lying in the small office in their home shortly after 3:30 P.M., when she returned from a shopping trip. She remembers looking at her watch, and noting the time. Her younger daughter, Lynn, was not due home from school for another ten minutes, so rather than wait at the end of the long driveway, Fran drove up to the house. Marlys's car was there, as she expected. Nothing was unusual.

Fran remembers every detail of the events that followed. As she went into the house through the unlocked ground-level door, she called to Marlys. She remembers noticing that the family St. Bernard, Patience, did not come bounding up to greet her but thought that Marlys must have let her out. (Later, Patience was found upstairs, closed in Fran's bedroom, where she would have gone to avoid anyone who came into the house who was not close family. The killer apparently was able to shut the door and confine the dog.)

Fran thought Marlys was on the phone when Marlys didn't answer her. Fran remembers that she was carrying a package, her purse, and some mail she had picked up in town. She remembers putting the package and her purse down on the stairs to the second floor and walking toward the small office. She remembers noticing that the door to a spare room was open. The door had been closed when Fran left home that morning. (The killer apparently was able to hide in that room until Marlys went into the office.)

Fran will never forget the scene in the office. Marlys sat slumped back against the wall, facing the huge rolltop desk that held the mail, which she had put there in what was probably her last conscious act. Her unopened purse had fallen at her feet.

Fran immediately called the ambulance through the Washington County sheriff's dispatcher. She remembers being calm and clear in her description and directions, but not calm in expressing her urgency. She remembers shouting to the sheriff when he arrived to use the side door because the front door was locked.

Fran tried to give Marlys first aid as she waited for the ambulance crew to arrive. They were soon on the scene and rushed Marlys to receive emergency treatment.

Fran also called a friend—me. I have since become her husband. At about 3:45 P.M., I received a phone call in my office in Minneapolis. That call and the haunting voice I heard still come back to me, never to be forgotten. "Jack! Oh, Jack! If I ever needed you, I need you now. It's Marlys. It's bad. Come now. Don't wait."

After talking just long enough to know where to go, I drove as fast as I could to Fran's home. The ambulance was going west as I drove east. I saw it on its way to the hospital as I raced toward Afton. Fran and I met a short distance from her house; she was in another car being taken to the emergency room. She moved to my car and began to describe the horror of finding Marlys.

Marlys never had a chance. Fran told me that in the car. The doctors said that as well. Two days later, on Thursday, May 10,

1979, Marlys was officially declared dead and her wish to be an organ donor was honored.

The murder is still unsolved.

1 GRIEF IS NEVER OVER

Grief is a pain you cannot physically touch. It is a pain of emptiness, as when an arm has been amputated. You know your arm has been cut off, and you don't think about its being gone every minute of the day. But it's still gone. You can live with the loss; in fact, you can live a fairly complete life without your arm, but you can't ever expect life to be the way it was before.

It was a long time before Fran could shut her eyes and not see Marlys lying as she found her. Fran has come to accept that the murder may never be solved and the killer may never be punished by a court of law. She has come to accept a lot of things. She has even come to accept that Marlys is dead. She has learned to live with her grief, as the pain comes much less often and is, perhaps, less intense. But she will never stop missing Marlys.

Fran says her faith in God has kept her sane. It has not been easy. And it is a fair question to ask how faith has helped her move beyond grieving and stay sane, because for some people religion is not an answer to this awful grief. We have searched the Hebrew scriptures, the New Testament, and religious writings by people of many faiths, but there is no magic verse or saying that takes away the pain of this kind of loss. No religious doctrine helps a person fully understand these feelings. Fran asked many times, "Where is God in all this?"

Yet Fran does get comfort from her faith. She realizes she cannot survive this terrible loss alone. She needed help then, and she needs it now, and she always will.

One source of help can be the comfort found in personally meaningful verses of scripture. These verses are special because they give comfort, joy, or contentment. The truth they contain for us resonates with the understanding that we draw from life experiences.

We learned one such verse from a friend, a pastor, a man who deals with the grief and pain of the homeless and the victims of war in Nicaragua. When grief and its accompanying pain are too much for the moment, he walks. As he walks, he recites and sometimes sings aloud his own rhythmical version adapted from Isaiah 61:3:

> He gave me beauty for ashes,
> the oil of joy for mourning,
> a garment of praise
> for the spirit of heaviness.
> I am a tree of righteousness,
> a planting of the Lord,
> that he might be glorified.

Neither of us can read, recite, or even think about this verse—or sing it as our friend taught us—without feeling a bit better.

Scripture may not give us specific answers to the questions that we want to ask. It may not tell us why Marlys was murdered. It won't explain the actions of the killer in terms we understand. It won't explain why some children get cancer and others don't. But we are comforted, and that is the beginning of healing.

A friend, a professor of theology whose son was killed by a drunken driver, admitted to me, "There are no answers to some questions, but you know that. You are a fellow traveler." Fellow travelers reach out to each other, accompany each other when the need is greatest. They do not let the lack of concrete, understandable answers prevent the healing process from beginning. My friend offers compassion, not easy answers, and in that offering both he and I find comfort.

The theology of accompaniment acknowledges that fellow travelers want to help each other begin to heal and reduce the pain of their grief. By reaching out, by simply being there for others, healing begins. Grief-stricken and tormented souls slowly become aware that others are with them. In time, even without answers, they begin to want to be healed, taking that first step which leads to additional steps and healing.

A story in John 5:2–9 has helped us to understand the importance of wanting to be healed.

> Now in Jerusalem by the Sheep Gate there is a pool, called in Hebrew Beth-zatha, which has five porticoes. In these lay many invalids— blind, lame, and paralyzed. One man was there who had been ill for thirty-eight years. When Jesus saw him lying there and knew that he had been there a long time, he said to him, "Do you want to be made well?" The sick man answered him, "Sir, I have no one to put me into the pool when the water is stirred up; and while I am making my way, someone else steps down ahead of me." Jesus said to him, "Stand up, take your mat and walk." At once the man was made well, and he took up his mat and began to walk.

Now that day was a sabbath! This scripture comforts us not by leading us to believe there will be a miracle. The expectation of the sick man is not that his paralysis will be cured. He was lying there, waiting for the impossible, when Jesus came to him, asking if he wanted to be healed. Certainly, for parents who read these verses, there is no promise that the child who has died will be given back to them. Their hope comes from knowing that healing is something that has to be wanted. The question that is asked is, "Do you want to be made well?"

Fran's father died suddenly when she was nine years old. She prayed then for God to bring him back to life. "I begged, pleaded, bargained, and cried," Fran says, "and my father did not come back." When Marlys was murdered, she prayed again for God to answer her prayer and give her back. Once more, she begged, pleaded, bargained, and cried. Marlys did not come back.

In time, Fran realized that praying for miracles was not going to help her deal with her grief. Of course she wanted Marlys back; she always will. But now she admits that, in this world, it doesn't happen. Fran wanted to be healed. She didn't— and doesn't—want to be paralyzed by her grief, wanting only the return of her daughter. Fran was able to say, "If Marlys can't come back to me, I want to be healed."

But it was not until Fran found others who had experienced the tragedy of the death of a child that she started to heal. Real healing began when she started to help others.

Fran is not an expert. She has not been trained in grief counseling. "I don't have all the answers," she admits, "but I do know one thing. Grief is never over. It only erupts less frequently as time goes on."

2 WHEN REALITY FINALLY HITS

Intense grief brings intense pain to those who mourn. The death of a child brings grief that comes like ocean waves in a ferocious storm. At first, the pain is unbearable, and then it gets worse.

The initial pain a parent feels when a child dies is buried beneath the shock. As the shock wears off, the pain can be hidden in denial or absorbed in anger. In time, when you accept your child's death as a fact, when you face it with acceptance—or at least resignation—the pain feels worse. After shock, anger, and denial have ceased to act as protection from reality, the pain is still there.

After Marlys was attacked, the ambulance crew rushed her to the emergency room. There was so much confusion. Fran was disoriented and in shock. As reality began to penetrate, she began to experience unbearable pain. That was just the beginning.

Fran realizes now that during the first couple of years after Marlys was murdered, she endured many kinds of pain. For example, whenever she closed her eyes, she would see Marlys as she first found her, on the floor in a pool of blood. She thought she would never be able to erase this vision from her mind. Going to bed became torture because it meant closing her eyes. Stopping to think about a task she was doing without thought, just to occupy her mind, brought the paralyzing sight back. How could she pray when just closing her eyes brought back the pain her prayers were intended to heal?

Even when the vision became less frequent, the certainty that it would come back brought fear of that remembered pain. Even now, more than sixteen years after Marlys's murder, the vision comes once in a while. Those are the bad days, but they are not every day anymore.

It is important for the bereaved to know that healing does take place. There will be times when sleep will come without pain and concentration will return so that necessary work can be done and even fun things can take place. A time will come again when prayer is a comfort and a reminder that God has been present and active in the healing process.

It is important for others, for those who would offer beauty for ashes and the oil of joy for mourning, to realize that time for healing belongs to the bereaved. The rest of the world cannot see the visions of horror. Others don't have the ability to let in the pain. It is the task of other people to be understanding even though they have no real understanding. It is not easy to comfort those who mourn. It is not easy to understand pain you don't experience. The time for healing really does belong to the grieving parent who is feeling the pain. It belongs to the bereaved.

The hospital emergency room was chaotic. Marlys was already in surgery, and Fran was just starting to realize the full horror of what had happened. I had not seen Marlys or the pool of blood. I was trying to stop rejecting the words I was hearing. A barrier had already formed between us. Marlys's imminent death was a reality. Fran's pain was just beginning for her. There was no way for me to understand.

The hospital was so real. The doctors were absorbed with

trying to save Marlys. The police, who wanted statements from everybody, were no less serious than the doctors. Murder is as real as anything in life, and yet it was so hard to understand.

Many times since then, we have talked about how hard it is to accept a tragedy. Fran's call for help is still vivid in my memory, but at that time I couldn't comprehend the words. We both clearly remember the ride to the hospital—or, rather, we remember talking.

"There is no hope," Fran said.

"You don't know that. The doctors will do all they can." I tried to reason with her.

"You didn't see her. I did! I'll probably always see her like that. There was bone, and blood, and parts of her."

Fran wasn't crying as she spoke. That would come later. She was still trying to comprehend what her eyes had seen. She was having her first experience with the difficulty she would have in getting others to see what she saw.

I was offering comfort, but from a perspective that could not equal hers. I had not seen what Fran saw and I could not, even if I had been in the little office with Fran when Marlys was found. And, being blind, I first experienced the difficulty I would have in understanding the words I heard.

The barrier that was built that day without our knowledge has been almost completely lowered. But it took time. We speak of it ironically now, saying that understanding is almost possible for those who have not felt the pain of a bereaved parent, and those bereaved parents almost believe that others do understand. Eventually I did understand, but it required sacrificial caring. The hardest thing I have ever done was to bring into my heart and mind the realization that Marlys was dead, never again in this life ever to be here with us. It has taken Fran almost as long to believe me. For a long time, it was not my loss, not my daughter, not my pain, but Marlys has been missing from my life too, and Fran and I have shared that pain. Now we share the understanding as we share the memories.

What Fran remembers most about the hospital is the kindness of the nurses and doctors. It seemed to her that there were a dozen of them, doing what they could to comfort her as she watched the monitors, looking for a sign of hope. Teams of specialists worked hard and Fran remembers how caring they were as they explained each step, each option, each significant event. Fran remembers the hospital staff as a comfort and even more than a comfort. The staff was a physical support for her, keeping her in some condition to deal with the steps being taken, the results, and the lack of medical progress.

By the second day, it became clear that there was no hope. Marlys would never recover. She was brain dead. Nothing could be done to restore her to active life. Even then, the doctors and staff were a calming influence as they worked to prepare Marlys for becoming a donor.

The fact that Marlys would be a donor was important to Fran. She and Marlys had talked about that possibility, and Marlys had placed the donor authorization on her driver's license when she reached the age of eighteen. She had known this act would give life and hope to others.

Fran still remembers that time in the hospital. "I was like a zombie, unable to function. The pain was unbearable at first. I remember the hard work of the hospital staff as they prepared Marlys to be a donor, after there was no hope at all. Psalm 23 says, 'Thy rod and thy staff, they comfort me.' In my case, 'The hospital staff, they comforted me.' Looking back, I find God in that comfort."

3 Rescue from Unbearable Pain

The experiences of grief are jagged and erratic during the first years after a child dies. And grieving parents respond in many ways. They become distracted and unable to focus on day-to-day life; they feel loneliness, sadness, helplessness, despair; they suffer physical symptoms of illness; they sob; they feel shock; they deny the event. They may tell the story over and over again. They suffer confusion, anxiety, panic attacks, and severe depression. Some are trapped into bargaining with God, praying for their child's return in exchange for whatever they can imagine God would take. They also feel envy, frustration, resentment, bitterness, and hatred. All of these feelings occur, sometimes over and over.

But the greatest constant is the pain that comes from simply missing this child, the person who was loved so much.

The difficulty in being able to express feelings of grief is universal. No one can really feel these emotions for another person. In fact, when parents of a child who has died try to talk with each other about what they feel, they often will find they are at different places in their grieving. Each spouse is so consumed by individual feelings, there may be no room for extending comfort to the other. That must come later, as they discover similarities in their healing process.

At the moment of the death of a child—no matter what the

cause—the mind slams shut. Defenses are raised instinctively as the mind protects itself. This initial refusal to accept visible truth is automatic. It is a reflex, like blinking your eyes when confronted with a sudden bright light. The mind lets the data in only slowly, through filters such as shock and denial, rationalization and unconcern.

It is natural that people try to protect themselves from most of the horror in the world. Otherwise, everyone would be paralyzed by the hopelessness and tragedy that so many endure. Equally as bad, we would become numb, calloused, and unconcerned about the suffering of others. It is also natural, then, that those closest to the tragedy of a child's death are the most affected. And those who have compassion, those who have been hurt by similar pain, seek to accompany those newly bereaved, offering a presence of understanding by their accompaniment.

For some, if the tragedy is not personal, the barriers that are erected to keep out the pain of death may never come down. This is where the difference between a bereaved parent and someone less personally touched by the death—a co-worker or a neighbor—becomes obvious. Only the parent must live with the tragedy long enough to let the reality of the horror come fully into the mind, past the barriers of protection. Parents do not have the resources to protect themselves.

Fran saw the violence that hit Marlys. I learned about it soon, and others learned about it not much later. Everyone's mind slammed shut because the horror was too much to let in. Fran had to deal with it because she was closest to Marlys, who would never be home again. Over the days, weeks, and years of healing, the memory is accepted in a place in the mind where it can be looked at, not directly but with perspective. I had to deal with it because I chose to be with Fran, to marry her and remain part of her life.

Marlys wasn't my natural child; she wasn't part of me physically, but I knew her. We were planning a surprise Mother's Day party for Fran. If I was not vulnerable as a natural parent, the horror penetrated my mind and brought me great pain nevertheless. This is true for adoptive parents and stepparents who live with their children and love them as deeply as any natural parent. Just as the pain is so intense because we love our child so much, that same love is what lets us eventually heal and seek to help others.

After the initial early response of grief and offers to help, relatives and friends usually begin to pick up their own lives. Parents are often left to deal with their grief alone. Co-workers, friends, neighbors, and sometimes even family members avoid them or do not talk about the child's death.

Few people are able to help a parent or to understand what this parent is going through in trying to survive the loss of a child. The parent is deprived of the child's presence and feels that deeply. Shock is nature's way of softening the blow. Shock serves as a cushion, giving time to absorb the fact of loss. The parent hears words of comfort and sympathy about the death offered by others but can't comprehend their meaning, sometimes not until much later when friends are gone.

It takes time to believe what has happened. The denial stage may go on for weeks—or even longer. Each day at the time Marlys would have been coming home, Fran looked for her to appear. She would see a person who looked like Marlys walking down the street or at a shopping mall, only to realize that it was another young girl; it couldn't be Marlys. Fran tells of one particularly difficult time: "One day I followed a white Datsun B-210 like Marlys had because the girl driving it looked just like Marlys. When this car stopped at the post office, the reality hit me again, because that was where Marlys would go. It wasn't Marlys, of course."

Time slowly but eventually begins to build detours around the paths of painful memories, safeguarding happiness and blocking the pain. But so much time is needed before this happens. What is the difference between parents' grief and the sorrow of others? Why do parents and loved ones take so long to heal from grief that is, in fact, just as unacceptable to mere acquaintances or even strangers? Why are some people impatient for the grieving parent to get on with life? Why do some people seem to be so insensitive toward those still obviously in pain? Is there any hope for those who do not understand the pain of grief? Who has the right even to ask that they understand?

These questions need to be addressed, not so we can understand the behavior of friends and acquaintances but so bereaved parents can learn to cope with the apparent insensitivity of others and not suffer more from what seems to be lack of care and concern. We need to look at these questions, because those who have been hurt by tragedy have to be protected from those who can't understand. More than that, there is a need to open the eyes of those who no longer try to understand with compassion, who no longer have time for the suffering of those who are afflicted.

Consider the words of Paul in 2 Corinthians 1:8–10

> We do not want you to be unaware, brothers and
> sisters, of the affliction we experienced in Asia; for we
> were so utterly, unbearably crushed that we despaired of
> life itself. Indeed, we felt that we had received the sen-
> tence of death so that we would rely not on ourselves
> but on God who raises the dead. He who rescued us
> from so deadly a peril will continue to rescue us; on him
> we have set our hope that he will rescue us again.

Perhaps Paul survived an attack on his own person, but in those days of the early Christian church, and of the Jewish church as well, there were many, many mothers and fathers whose children died—violently. Paul was aware of these grieving parents. This is the kind of message a bereaved parent may want to send: We don't want you to be unaware of the affliction we experienced in Minnesota, for we were so utterly, unbearably crushed that we despaired of life itself.

The pain our family endured because of Marlys's death, and the pain others have endured because their son or daughter died, is enough so that all bereaved parents can, like Paul, claim to be "so utterly, unbearably crushed that [they] despaired of life itself."

This is reality, and from this reality they have a right to ask for the same comfort that Paul received. They understand the pain of those in both the New Testament and in the Hebrew scriptures. What they don't understand as easily is how God delivered them from their unbearable pain. It is time to look to God for some answers, for as Paul determines in 2 Corinthians 1:10, "He who rescued us from so deadly a peril will continue to rescue us; on him we have set our hope that he will rescue us again."

4 I NEED GOD NOW!

At a funeral, when scripture is read, sermons are preached, and prayers are offered, we understand that the one who has died is not being comforted. The funeral service is for those who are left behind. It allows those who are left with the reality of life after a loved one has died to honor, pay their respects, and mourn. It is a time for comforting one another, using many forms—music, sympathy, companionship, scripture, prayer—that express our hopes for healing. Yet the bereaved are not always able to respond immediately and to the degree that others expect. They are not always able to hear or feel what is being said or done because of the intensity of their grief.

A pastor, priest, rabbi, or friend may, before the funeral, console the family of the deceased, perhaps by reading prayers or scripture. In many cases, however, the memorial service or funeral is often the first time that any sort of religious words are spoken. It is now that scripture is read with the intention of bringing God's word to those present. Passages are spoken that illustrate the legitimate expectation of people seeking comfort from God. "My loved one has died and I seek comfort now." We look into the eyes of the speaker and hear, "Thy rod and thy staff, they comfort me."

In a religious service, focusing on words that promise comfort

and hope and invoking God's own words and name raise expectations that the words will, in fact, comfort the bereaved.
Depending upon the religious background and affiliation of the
mourners, the words may be familiar ones that have been heard
many times and even memorized, or they may be unfamiliar
words, invoking new thoughts and new ideas.

For those who have an extensive religious background or
training, old promises from scripture will be remembered. For
those whose background is not in the church, scripture's promises
may be heard for the first time. In both cases, the mourner will
hear words that give rise to certain expectations. This is the time
when people say, "If I ever needed God, I need God now!"

The death of a child brings trauma to the entire community,
and many people offer consolation. There was a viewing at the
funeral home for Marlys; the long line of friends and relatives
extended outside. The casket was closed because of her injuries;
her framed high school senior picture was placed on top. Fran
has the guest register, and she is amazed at the many names she
finds there, people who came to pay their respects. She doesn't
remember much of what happened. Picking the hymns for the
funeral seemed to be very important; she still remembers the
comfort they gave her that day, just knowing that familiar
expressions of faith were being sung.

People tried to comfort her as well. A viewing is a time when
people offer individual comfort to the bereaved. Everyone who
comes bears his or her own grief to some degree, and each person extends sympathies to the family and close friends. At the
viewing for Marlys, the young people were kind to Fran in a way
one could not anticipate. She says, "I remember all the kids even
now, so many years later. I remember those who had kind words
for me.

"But I don't remember much more. Lots of people were there, and I don't remember them. I remember sitting and speaking with people. I remember going through the motions. I had to see these people but I didn't want to see them, even though I know now they were trying to help, to share the sorrow. The doctor had given me a mild sedative. These were the most horrible days of my life. Only much later did I recognize that somehow those who were there were helping me just to survive."

The funeral was on Saturday morning. There was a procession, by car, from the funeral home in Stillwater to Memorial Lutheran Church in Afton. Cars following in the procession were in a line that seemed to have no end as they drove along the St. Croix River that Marlys loved. Fran remembers the line of cars. I remember that it rained.

Marlys's service was intended to celebrate her return to the Lord whom she loved and in whom she believed. The service was to remember her. But for Fran and the family and friends who gathered in that little white church, Marlys's service was also a chance for us to ask for comfort and to look to God for answers.

The service was led by Marlys and Fran's pastor, the Reverend Richard Borgstrom. Everyone was offered a chance to speak. Pastor Borgstrom read a poem that Fran's daughter, Lynn, then age sixteen, wrote on the day Marlys died.

Pastor Borgstrom delivered a message, based on scripture, that offered comfort to the family and friends who had packed the church to overflowing. He spoke clearly of the promise of victory over death in Jesus Christ. He spoke of the joy that Marlys has in being with God. He also spoke of the compassion that God offers those who mourn.

Pastor Borgstrom also spoke of his inability to find words to explain Marlys's murder and of the impossibility of explaining

or justifying much of the evil in the world. And he acknowledged that he didn't have all the answers.

After the funeral service, the casket was lowered into the
grave at the cemetery next to the church. More prayers were spoken. Fran says, "I started looking to God, beginning with the
church service, I guess, and have continued to look to God.
Over the years I have found that my faith in God is stronger
now than ever." Fran was given assurances in the form of scriptures, hymns, and a worship service that focused the presence of
God in our lives through our faith and through the church.
These assurances didn't take away all the pain, nor did they
ignore the pain that she felt. But the presence of God was
acknowledged, and that is a place from which healing can take
place.

Reality comes into people's lives, violently sometimes and
with finality, so they can no longer hold on to abstract ideas
about how life should be. Promises are no longer enough in the
face of violent reality, unless one can see how these promises are
going to be kept. Grief from the loss of a child brings unbearable pain, and the words of scripture do not immediately ease
that pain.

Even if we can concentrate on written or spoken words, it is
so hard to apply them to our own experience. Often, reality
intrudes in a life or a family or a nation in such a way that words
of God do not comfort sufficiently. Immediate events have so
much power and control over us that we seek more than comfort. We ask God for answers. "God, why did you let this happen? Why didn't you do something, God?"

To deny this legitimate crying out for answers is to hide
from real life and to prevent any possible recovery based upon
faith. It is essential to ask God for answers. To do otherwise is to

ignore God. Worse, to do otherwise is to deny ourselves the opportunity to have answers so that we can be healed. Those who ask God for answers, and who do not expect simple answers to very complicated questions, will find answers to those questions.

At a memorial service, scripture can comfort those who are alive, to reassure them of a future. One often-used reading is John 14:2–3:

> In my Father's house there are many dwelling
> places. If it were not so, would I have told you that I go
> to prepare a place for you? And if I go and prepare a
> place for you, I will come again and will take you to
> myself, so that where I am, there you may be also.

As we read that text, and as we look into the eyes of the bereaved, we hear the parent say, "Yes, my child is with Jesus even now, but why does it hurt so much?"

What about the pain the parents suffer, at the funeral and for days, weeks, years afterward? Isn't it reasonable to expect that scripture will give comfort, words that will ease the pain, even take it away?

Expectations of comfort are contradicted, however, by the death of the child, as by the death of a spouse, or by starvation in Ethiopia, or death squads in El Salvador, or Jesus on the cross. Genesis 1:31 says, "God saw everything that he had made, and indeed, it was very good."

How can what we experience be good? Parents ask, "How, God, am I comforted by you going to prepare rooms for us? How does that take away my pain, even if Marlys is in one of those rooms? Is it so much nicer than the room I gave her?"

5 LOOK TO THE INTERESTS OF OTHERS

In the pain of the loss of a child, deep-felt grief leads to difficult questions. What is fair? Why is there this evil? How could God allow this to happen? What did I do to cause, or even deserve, this pain? Why did it have to be my child? These are some of the questions that parents ask. To understand the answer we offer, we believe it is necessary to look to God. We have found you must believe in God in order to ask the hard questions of God. Even if you are filled with anger, pain or depression, the first step is to admit that God exists. If a grieving parent, out of anger or pain or depression, denies that God exists, it will not be possible for the parent to ask God the questions that need to be asked.

But how does one look to God for answers in the midst of grief when it is hard even to feel God's presence? This is done not by any special words but by understanding the life and humanity of Jesus Christ and the comfort of the Holy Spirit. Be assured, it is not much easier for someone who already has strong faith to seek answers than it is for someone with little or no faith.

All children have meaning for their parents. And out of the affirmation that this child did not live without meaning, and did not die a meaningless death, comes the affirmation that God provides an answer to our questions. To find this meaning, we look to the life of Jesus Christ and the meaning that Christ's life has for today.

How can we understand Jesus Christ? Are there words that summarize his life and humanity so as to give meaning to our child's life? We can begin with Paul's words in Philippians 2:1–8, which he wrote as a way to help the church in Philippi understand from the life of Jesus Christ the source of his answers.

> If then there is any encouragement in Christ, any consolation from love, any sharing in the Spirit, any compassion and sympathy, make my joy complete: be of the same mind, having the same love, being in full accord and of one mind. Do nothing from selfish ambition or conceit, but in humility regard others as better than yourselves. Let each of you look not to your own interests, but to the interests of others. Let the same mind be in you that was in Christ Jesus, who, though he was in the form of God, did not regard equality with God as something to be exploited, but emptied himself, taking the form of a slave, being born in human likeness. And being found in human form, he humbled himself and became obedient to the point of death—even death on a cross.

Paul admonishes us to look to the interests of others, not just our own. He holds up Jesus Christ as an example, as he became human and in human form suffered death on a cross. Jesus gave his life because he humbled himself and was obedient. We also are to humble ourselves and be obedient.

This is the answer bereaved parents receive as they struggle with the pain and grief of the death of their child. The parent is admonished to look to the others. The parent is told that it is necessary to be humble and even to die.

What kind of answer is this? How can obedience and humility be of value at such a time? As we continue to live with our pain and our loss and our grief, are we comforted by an understanding of Jesus Christ that suggests we must suffer as well? Are we to die too?

The answer to these questions has two parts. The first part is, Yes, we must be willing to die in order to have comfort in our pain. The second part of the answer is, We are not to die for ourselves, because there is no obedience or humility in that. Instead, we must be willing to die for others. We will lose our pain to the extent that we live for others and, if we must, die for them.

We need to understand that although our pain is unbearable to us initially, others have borne similar pain, and others will bear pain after us. This understanding comes from the two ways we view and experience suffering. The first is existential, viewing suffering and pain from within, as a participant. The second is intellectual, viewing suffering and pain from without, as an observer. When we can see that others have the pain we have experienced, we seek to comfort them. When we seek to comfort them, we are comforted.

Fran has found a poem that says it another way. The poem explores the struggle for healing and the discovery that healing can take place. It was written by Barbara Williams, a nurse and bereaved parent who wrote this poem after a night spent comforting another bereaved parent.

From comfort that the poem gives, and its understanding of the feelings of a bereaved parent, it is clear that the author is also one who grieves and who has experienced healing.

Stepping Stones

Come, take my hand, the road is long. We must
travel by stepping stones. No, you're not alone. I'll go

with you. I know the road well, I've been there. Don't fear the darkness. I'll be with you. We must take one step at a time. But remember we may have to stop awhile. It is a long way to the other side and there are many obstacles.

We have many stones to cross. Some are bigger than others . . . shock, denial, and anger to start. Then comes guilt, despair, and loneliness. It's a hard road to travel but it must be done. It's the only way to reach the other side.

Come, slip your hand in mine. What? Oh, yes, it's strong. I've held so many hands like yours. Yes, mine was one time small and weak like yours. Once, you see, I had to take someone's hand in order to take the first step. Oops! you've stumbled. Go ahead and cry. Don't be ashamed, I understand. Let's wait here awhile and get your breath. When you're stronger we'll go on, one step at a time. There's no need to hurry.

Say, it's nice to hear you laugh. Yes, I agree, the memories you shared are good. Look, we're halfway there now; I can see the other side. It looks so warm and sunny. Oh, have you noticed? We're nearing the last stone and you're standing alone. And look, your hands, you've let go of mine, and we've reached the other side.

But wait. Look back. Someone is standing there. They are alone and want to cross the stepping stones. I better go; they need my help. What? Are you sure? Why, yes; I'll wait. You know the way—you've been there. Yes, I agree—it's your turn, my friend—to help someone else across the stepping stones.

This poem speaks beautifully about helping others over to the other side, across denial, despair, and loneliness, and ends with the desire to help another rather than to be helped. This is the answer: It is not until the bereaved think of others more than of themselves that they begin to heal.

I will say more about this later, but the key word is "others." When a bereaved parent, grandparent, or sibling responds to God's call to love others who need help on the stepping stones, healing begins. This joint process of being healed and healing others is the answer that comes from looking to God for answers.

How does knowing there is a God to whom we may address questions help a bereaved parent? How is this an answer if the parent of the child has faith? What about the conflict between expectation—of comfort—and experience—pain? The answer, as I have said, is not found in a few words but in the merger of our pain with the pain of others, in the life and humanity of Jesus Christ.

Christ lived on earth for many years in order to give us that example. Any healing that is said to be immediate is contrary to the expectations of many and to the experiences of everyone. The stepping stones are far apart. It is not until we can help others that we are helped in our pain.

How long until we are helped? How long has it taken even to remember that there are others?

6 HELP THESE SUFFERING PEOPLE

At first, because of the shock and pain, people in the early stages of grief scarcely notice the others around them. They barely remember who was at the funeral or memorial service. They forget who brought a meal to feed the rest of the family. But after a time they ask, What can I do when I am in so much pain and no one really wants to listen to me? Many people whom we would expect to behave otherwise run away from bereaved people and try to avoid contact with them, even when they are aware of their responsibility to help.

Ministers, rabbis, and priests may stay away because they know the bereaved is in pain and they don't know what to say. The clergy are aware of times when they have tried to say something but what they said was the wrong thing. Every clergy person and counselor has stories of saying the wrong thing.

Estimates suggest that a large number of parents who lose a child drop out of church. The largest single reason that these parents drop out of church is mistakes made by the minister, rabbi, or priest.

The second largest reason why parents drop out of church is the congregation. They offer no oil of joy for mourning, because they too do not know what to say. Finally, friends and relatives may mean well but say the wrong thing also. These people do not intend to isolate or harm the grieving parents. They just do not know what to say.

27

Often, in such relationships, parents' pain and hurt build up and, instead of healing, greater stress occurs in a marriage. Grief-related organizations have learned that many parents of children who have died are divorced in the first few years after the loss. Some spouses claim that the divorce was going to happen anyway, but often this is rationalization, transferring pain and its cause to one's mate. Sometimes this pain is also transferred to other children or to one's own parents or in-laws.

The tragedy of all this transfer of anger is that it could be prevented, or at least limited. If friends and family would talk together and try to express how they feel, perhaps they would not make the pain worse. Perhaps the time they spent together would be healing instead of harmful.

It is fair to want to know what to say to those who are in such great pain. It is fair for them to want to know why no one will talk with them. It is important that people communicate during the early time of grief, and so it is important to find out what to say.

Much of the behavior that damages or ruins relationships can be prevented. There are two general guidelines to keep in mind at all times. Whether one is clergy or spouse or friend, neither is easy. First, it is important to listen to the bereaved, listen long after you think that no more needs to be said. Second, if you have to talk, don't say the wrong thing.

Talking with a bereaved parent is difficult sometimes, so the first recommendation, listening long after you think there is no more that needs to be said, will be hard. But it is necessary if you are going to help the parent recover. People who suppress their grief are often in a continual state of stress and shock. They are unable to move beyond that state. Grief that stays locked up inside a person can actually change or destroy that person, as a poison does that is not flushed out of the system. You may think that persons who do not appear to be grieving are not in fact grieving. But that is not true. The suffering is probably taking another form.

Grieving people suffer physical effects from the shock and trauma of the death of a loved one. The stress comes out in high blood pressure, ulcers, cancer, and many other body ailments. It is important to be able to help these suffering people so they will not destroy their bodies, their marriages, their careers. In Fran's early stages of grief, she experienced many physical problems. She had paralysis, shortness of breath, and pains; as she says, "I had just about everything you could imagine, and at times I thought I was going crazy." Fran has found that her experiences are quite common.

The stress is more than physical; it often leads to emotional and psychological difficulties. Fran was left with a sense of unreality. She had a strong sense of guilt as a survivor. Events were complicated by involvement with medical and legal authorities. Her need to blame someone was extremely strong, particularly since the murder was not solved. She was left with a sense of helplessness and at times exhibited high levels of agitation. Like so many bereaved parents, she regrets things not said and activities not done with Marlys. To this day, she struggles with trying to understand why Marlys was murdered. These feelings are also very common and are experienced by almost everyone at one time or another.

Sometimes, the terrible feelings and the stress overshadow the fact that there is a real need to talk and be talked to. It is important that those who would offer comfort be physically present as well as emotionally supportive, no matter what the grieving parent may say.

The overriding principle of grief ministry is just simply being there for the bereaved. It is so important not to allow your grieving friends to remain isolated. Remember that you can reach out to these people even though you cannot take away the pain. You can help them to tolerate what they are going through. Let your genuine concern and caring show. Try gently to plant the seeds of hope that some day the pain will decrease. Listen without being judgmental.

Bereaved parents may not be able to say clearly what they want in the way of support. This does not mean, however, that the bereaved do not have certain very real, even strong, expectations. Studies show that the bereaved want others to comfort them, particularly others who have been there and really understand. But even those who don't have an experience of this magnitude to draw on can respond to the expectations of the grieving person by being present and by listening.

It is good to allow the bereaved to cry and to encourage them to continue crying if they show signs of starting. They expect you to understand that they need to cry—that they are adult, mature, and well-adjusted, but that this is too much to bear alone.

Let the bereaved friend or family member tell the story, over and over and over. Do not be amazed if grievers repeatedly talk about many of the same things. They expect to be able to express their feelings and will be hurt if you do not let them do so. Both of you will find confidence in knowing that talking, and repeating, is normal.

This is all part of the healing process. Fortunately, Pastor Borgstrom told me at the funeral that I would have to listen and listen again and that I should always appear to be interested. Many times I had to remember those words, and, yes, sometimes I forgot.

Parents also expect you to mention their dead child's name often when talking with them. This is very important. We encourage the griever to talk about the deceased and their mutual relationship realistically. Be a long-term listener, not just on the first day or the first week but in the weeks and months to follow.

But recognize that if you start to listen, you will be expected to continue listening. You will not be expected to have the answer, just to listen. Even after a year, do not be afraid of silence and listening when you are with the bereaved person. If the bereaved is important enough to you that you began a listening relationship, that person is important enough to continue it.

Above all, let your bereaved friend set the time schedule for healing. Unless you have been there, you will not know how long it takes. If you *have* been there, you know it takes forever, but there are stages of healing. Let each person walk that journey at an individual pace, crossing the stepping stones one by one. And remember to be there, offering them a needed hand.

This principle of being there is fundamental to what Fran and I call the theology of accompaniment. There is a passage in the Gospel of Mark that describes this principle in action. The time is just before Jesus is taken to his death on the cross. The place is the garden of Gethsemane. From this text, it is clear that even Jesus' closest friends didn't understand what was happening; moreover, they didn't know what to do or say. The text illustrates some of the problems that are found by everyone who seeks to comfort someone who is suffering in a way and because of a reason that the comforter does not understand.

> They went to a place called Gethsemane; and he said to his disciples, "Sit here while I pray." He took with him Peter and James and John, and began to be distressed and agitated. And he said to them, "I am deeply grieved, even to death; remain here, and keep awake." And going a little farther, he threw himself on

the ground and prayed that, if it were possible, the hour might pass from him. He said, "Abba, Father, for you all things are possible; remove this cup from me; yet, not what I want, but what you want." He came and found them sleeping; and he said to Peter, "Simon, are you asleep? Could you not keep awake one hour? Keep awake and pray that you may not come into the time of trial; the spirit indeed is willing, but the flesh is weak." And again he went away and prayed, saying the same words. And once more he came and found them sleeping, for their eyes were very heavy; and they did not know what to say to him." (Mark 14:32–40)

How many times do well-meaning friends act just like Peter, James, and John? Jesus said he needed them to be there for him, and they could not even keep their eyes open. They did not have the energy to support their friend, especially since they didn't even understand why there was so much grief. They did not know what to say to him. Scripture does not record that Peter or James or John tried to say anything. Perhaps they had logical answers, and perhaps they said nothing.

In their times of trial, for Peter and John (in Acts 4) or for James and Peter (in Acts 12), perhaps Gethsemane was repeated. Perhaps having been with Jesus as he asked for accompaniment helped them. Most likely, they expected others to be there with them and to listen even if they had nothing to say.

Grieving parents need and expect others to be with them. They want to talk about what has happened. Their expectations can be met, but only when we are present. And those who sit with the bereaved need just as much as did Peter, James, and John to learn what to say at such a time.

For the most part, talking with the bereaved is a process of accompaniment, of being there. Those who genuinely want to help are trying not to fall asleep in the garden of Gethsemane or at the kitchen table, hearing the same story over and over and over again. What can they say?

As I noted earlier, at first the grieving person will not even know you are there. And yet your presence is the best thing you can offer. Healing is only just beginning when one can recognize the presence of others. Healing is only just starting when some small act of kindness breaks into the pain-shrouded emotional paralysis.

The grieving person notices that another person is present, in accompaniment, and the pain subsides, just a bit, just for a moment. The presence of another dimly enters the grieving one's mind. He or she is aware that a cup of tea has been placed nearby at the right time. Someone has picked up the other children from school; who performed that act of kindness? A faucet that drips has been fixed. Maybe the grass has been cut. Who has been so nice?

The one trying to reach the bereaved has not performed any magical act but, rather, has just been there, doing something the loved one might need, notice, and appreciate. These small acts of love and concern often start the healing.

7 THERE ARE NO EASY ANSWERS

As soon as a death occurs, many words are spoken in an attempt to console. Some things that are said are not comforting at all. Some words hurt, and others show lack of compassion. If the words are harmless enough, the grieving parent won't remember them. In fact, it is a generalization that those in the deep pain of the death of a child won't remember a word you say, unless you say the wrong thing.

Bereaved persons expect you to make an appropriate remark. They can respond with ease and seeming grace to what they expect. Even if what you say is true, there may be no reason to say it to those who are grieving over the death of their child. If they are newly bereaved, it will hurt them greatly. If they have begun to recover, you just might get a response that hurts you.

This part of the guidelines for talking with a bereaved parent is also built on the theology of accompaniment, of being there with the person in pain. The reason why you take the time to sit with someone in pain, and the reason why you seek words of comfort, has to be founded on love. It may not—indeed, often will not—be love of spouse or parent or friend, but it must be Christian love.

Clergy people speak of love for their flock. Certainly friends and family should show love above all else. This is not the time for answers, especially answers that purport to explain why or how a horrible event like the death of a child occurs. This is a time for love, for accompaniment, not for easy answers. Words that are spoken at this time must be based on love, not knowledge. At this time in the bereaved's healing, nothing is as important as love, and so the words must convey that love.

"Love" and particularly "Christian love" are words that might have different meanings for different people. What we mean here, and what is needed by the bereaved who are in so much pain, is unconditional love that is based upon compassion, not on understanding. This is, to us, the meaning behind the words of Paul in 1 Corinthians 13:1–2.

> If I speak in the tongues of mortals and of angels,
> but do not have love, I am a noisy gong or a clanging
> cymbal. And if I have prophetic powers, and understand
> all mysteries and all knowledge, and if I have all faith, so
> as to remove mountains, but do not have love, I am
> nothing.

Everything you say should be governed by this concept: This is not the time for answers, it is the time for love. Love is the foundation of accompaniment, the guiding light that prevents us from sounding like a noisy gong or a clanging cymbal. Love keeps us from saying the wrong thing.

You have probably heard someone say, "God wanted your child more than you did." Are they kidding? This is the voice of a clanging cymbal. Bereaved parents know that God has eternity to have their child, after they have had a chance to raise their child to adulthood and the adult has lived a good life. God can wait.

No matter what theological assumption forms the basis for such a statement, it is not love for someone to presume to know how much God wanted a child and, by saying that, actually ignore or deny how much the parent also wanted that child.

You may also have heard someone say, "You'll get over it in a few weeks." That remark is rooted in the observer's discomfort and naive hope. In fact, studies show that the pain of grief from the loss of a child is almost as strong on the first anniversary of the death as it is when the death occurred. On the anniversary, there is no shock for protection, and the reality is becoming clear. And that is just the first year. No more can the parent say, "Last year, my child and I were together at this time. Last year, we did this together."

In reality, who can say when another should be healed, or even be healing? Those who have not experienced the death of their own child have no idea how long it takes to get over it. Those who have had the experience know it takes forever to recover completely. A person is lucky to start healing in the first year.

Another remark people make in an attempt to console is, "You have" or can have "other children." But that is irrelevant. Each child is unique. Shared memories and emotions cannot be transferred like the title to a piece of property. Each child is part of the parent, and parents are not consoled over losing one part of themselves by the fact that they may someday have another part.

All children have the right to grow up in a loving relationship with their parents, even though that may not be the reality that a particular child experiences. It is unreasonable to ask one parent or child to substitute for another. This denies the individuality of the child who has died. Not only does this place a burden on the remaining children to become someone they cannot be, it prevents parents and children from helping one another in their grief.

Amazingly, some people say, "God is punishing you for something." Not only is this cruel, placing guilt on an already vulnerable person; it says that a child can be allowed to die as punishment for the sins of another. This trivializes the child's life just when the parents are seeking to find meaning in their child's death.

Such a statement is clearly lacking in love. It is also theologically arrogant to pretend to know what God would decide to do about a specific sin in the face of so much sin in the world. Of course, saying that God is punishing the *child* for some sin is no better, either as a comfort or as a theological position. It is best not to talk about sin in such a situation unless you are God or unless you are sinless!

Have you heard someone say, "Your child is better off with Jesus"? While it is true that being in the presence of God is wonderful, it is not loving to suggest that with the parent is not the natural and proper place for the child to be. Notice that the speaker does not volunteer his or her child to be with God at an age that is not natural. The grieving parent certainly notices that. How could you respond when the parent asks, "What kind of parent does that make me, if I can't make life nice enough for my child?" All bereaved parents we have ever met say their child is with God. But that doesn't stop the pain of their loss.

Have you been tempted to say, "We are only given what we can handle"? What does that mean? A parent's first calm reaction to that remark is to ask, "If I were weaker, would my child still be alive? If I am stronger, will God take my other children too?" Words like these are often spoken as the parent is on the verge of emotional or physical collapse. How can this give a parent the strength to continue, when to collapse might bring back the child?

Have you been tempted to say, "God has a plan"? Many people believe that God is in control of every event in every life. A parent who believes that has probably already had this thought. If the parent doesn't believe there is a plan, or isn't sure, now is not the time to get out the blueprint.

Grieving parents are not interested in hearing that God planned this grief, this pain that is the worst event in their life. Most, if not all, grieving parents would rather have died instead of their child. They will not find God or comfort in plans. You will be lucky if they only tell you, "It is time for Plan B."

A second text from the Bible is also used at times of grief. More often than not it is misquoted or misunderstood because it is not carefully read, and assumptions are made that are not based on what is written.

Paul's first letter to the Thessalonians (1 Thess. 5:16–18), says, "Rejoice always, pray without ceasing, give thanks in all circumstances; for this is the will of God in Christ Jesus for you." This text is misread at times to say, "give thanks *for* all circumstances," when the language is "give thanks *in* all circumstances." People are not exhorted by this scripture to give thanks for the fact that their child has died. Rather, and most important, they are urged to give thanks to God in these times of grief. They don't thank God for the death of their child, but they may thank God for the comfort they receive in their grief—if others don't say the wrong thing.

It is also important to see that "this is the will of God" refers to the "rejoicing," the "praying," the "giving thanks *in* all" and does not refer to specific events, be they tragic or joyous, particularly not to the death of a child.

The wrong thing should not be said. If what you are about to say to someone in grief offers an easy or simple answer, don't say it. There are no easy answers—there is only accompaniment.

The two things you need to remember, as one actively seeks to comfort or be comforted, are not difficult to remember. First, the person who needs to talk is the person experiencing the grief. Second, the person who is interested in helping should offer love, not advice or opinions.

Especially in the early stages of grief, all that can be said and all that can be heard is, "I'm sorry." If you have been there yourself, you can also say, "I understand." If you have not been there, all you can add is, "I'm here for you."

8 I'm Here for You

During the two days Marlys was in the hospital, and before the certainty of her death was accepted as fact, everyone involved experienced anger for the first time. Between Tuesday afternoon, when the ambulance arrived, and Thursday evening, when the arrangements were complete for Marlys to be an organ donor, all who were directly involved were angry at least once, as their very souls cried out in pain.

At the hospital, Fran was given a mild sedative and her extended family was called. Her son Raymond, who is two years older than Marlys, was one of the first to arrive. His anger at the unknown assailant, the murderer, and his frustration at not knowing who to be angry with was great. Several times, he was heard to shout, "It's my sister who is in there! Why can't I have an answer?"

This was a hard way for a twenty-year-old to take the last steps in growing up. It was a hard way for him to have to face death. Ray, like all young people, believed that if he were not immortal, at least he was going to live forever. He had not seen death before, except for the "natural" death of very old relatives. Like all the rest of us, Ray had been shocked by the violence, and he was angry.

His response was, "I'll kill the one who did it." In this he was joined by most of the friends and family who gathered at the hospital. Wanting to strike back at the person who causes such great pain is normal, and Ray did as well as any other young man with his anger. After all, his father and his maternal grandmother also said, "I'll kill the one who did it." No one does much better than this in coping with senseless death.

Before all the family was able to arrive at the hospital, the first of several misunderstandings occurred. In little ways, anger built. Some felt they should have called certain relatives but not others. Some wanted to argue with the doctors, and others became upset when the doctors wanted to talk to Fran and not to them. Some argued briefly about who was most hurt by Marlys's death.

But the most awful part was the first signs of suspicion. Who did this awful deed? Was it someone in the family? Where were you, someone asked, when it happened? Can you prove it? In the lack of knowledge about who could have committed the murder, anger led to suspicion. Those who were suspicious looked angrily at those they suspected and said, "I don't care who did it, I'll kill the murderer!"

Everyone whose child dies has great anger that somehow must be dealt with before peace can come. Where the cause is known, as in auto accidents or illness or in cases of violence where the perpetrator is known, the anger can be directed at a specific individual. Even when a doctor provides the best care that modern medicine is capable of, there is anger. Even when a driver is not drunk and has no way to prevent the accident, there is anger.

When a child commits suicide, that anger may be directed at the child. A father we know whose daughter took her own life with a gun she had secretly purchased still talks about how he screamed at her when he found her dying from the self-inflicted gunshot wound. There is anger.

Now, sixteen years later, we no longer speak of killing the one responsible for Marlys's murder. We are still angry, and this thought is deep in everyone's private thoughts, but we can talk about that anger and find some peace. Because our family is unable to vent our anger at a drunken driver or a careless doctor or any other known person, we know it is always there. But we still need to deal with the anger, some of us more than others.

For some of the family, it feels good to be angry at one person or another. For others in the family, the anger has somehow been eased. Forgiveness has been granted to the killer or at least the effort to forgive has been made. Some of them no longer need the emotional fuel of revenge, directed at real or imagined persons.

Fran said often, as she began the healing process, that if she couldn't have Marlys back, she wanted to be healed. We have talked about how the healing benefit that comes from saying that is not the same when we change the wording to focus on our anger. We talk about saying, "If I can't have Marlys back, I want to forgive the murderer." It doesn't have the same ring and doesn't sound like healing advice. But for us it is the alternative to anger. Do we want our anger to consume us? Do we want the murderer to claim another victim, destroying our lives as we burn in anger? We have said we do not. We want to be healed, and if we have to think forgiveness to this unknown murderer, it is better to do so than to let our lives be destroyed as well.

When the murder is solved—if it is—the anger will rage once again, stronger than at the time Marlys was killed. When the murderer is found, no matter what we have done until now, there will be anger. Someone will say again, "I'll kill that person!" We pray no one will actually try. We know this, however: Again there will be anger, and we will have to deal with it. And we pray that again we will be given the grace to seek healing.

Grief counselors say it is all right to be angry. Anger is a natural emotion, a natural response to death. Of course, the counselors are not giving permission to experience what is a natural reaction. They know it is necessary to have an outlet for the anger in order to return to a semblance of normality. Rather, the permission they give is to *express* the anger, to vent it, as it were, so that it does not dwell inside, causing physical and emotional damage. The pain of loss will always be with the bereaved parent. The anger must be dealt with, because if it is not it will cause more pain. The anger has to be expressed, and those who are around the grieving parent will, I hope, understand that the anger comes and has to come out. Other bereaved parents know this. Those who have not been there most often do not understand, and so they do not know what to say in the face of anger. We hope they will remember to say, "I'm here for you."

A way to forgive the unforgivable, even when there is no blame, has not been found. Many times, as the pain of the loss increases, as the protective layers of shock wear off, anger comes out that is directed toward those who are not responsible for the illness or accident or other tragedy that took the child unfairly from them. Partners may blame each other because they can't blame themselves. There is so much pain, and the anger is there. It is too late to understand, and even when one partner does understand, there often is not enough energy to care.

Anger is often directed at surviving children, both within and outside the family. Why should another child have a good life? My child is dead. There is anger, even when the angry one knows it is wrong.

One day a friend arrived at our house sobbing, unable to unbuckle her seat belt. One of her neighbors had brought her boy over for help in tying a bow tie for a tuxedo. It was prom weekend, five years after our friend's son Jon had been killed in an automobile accident.

The neighbor meant no harm. She was a good friend and knew Jon's parents go to formal affairs. Surely they could help. Jon's mother tied the tie, smiling all the while. She sent the neighbors on their way and drove over to us. The crying started before she arrived, as did the need to speak out in anger at an unfair life.

That is the kind of anger that the bereaved understand.

9 Being There Is the Only Help

Sooner or later, regardless of their religious faith, parents become angry at God. They rage, saying, "If God is so powerful, how could God let this happen to my child?" Or "If God is so good, how could God let this happen to my child?"

This conflict in our understanding of God's nature has led some to abandon hope in God. Rabbi Harold S. Kushner, who himself survived the death of his son, struggles with this conflict in his book *When Bad Things Happen to Good People* and proposes an answer. Rabbi Kushner describes his choice as being between an all-powerful God and a loving God and decides on a God of love. If God is all-powerful, God could have prevented the death of Kushner's child. If God is loving, God feels the pain that Kushner feels. Kushner would rather have a God who is sympathetic than a God who could prevent bad things and doesn't do so.

Many grieving family members make a similar choice in order not to abandon belief in God altogether. When their experiences do not coincide with their expectations about God, how can there be understanding? Part of the grieving process includes seeking understanding of God's role in our lives, and we can't leave God out of this struggle. Isn't Kushner saying that our experience of God is that God is not both all-powerful and loving? If God is not both, who can worship a God that could have saved our child but didn't? Who needs a loving God who can't bring back our dead child? I am uncomfortable with Kushner's logic that requires one to choose between two lesser visions of God. Just as the death of God's own son Jesus Christ is understood only in light of the resurrection, our understanding of God, of evil, and even of the death of our child also can be understood only in the light of the empty tomb.

For bereaved parents, the answer to these questions is found not in intellectual arguments but in the merger of one's pain with the pain of others, in the life and humanity of Jesus Christ. Help does not come from knowing that God is all-powerful or all-loving. It comes from the experience of helping others, of being present for others, eventually of being willing to give one's own life for others.

Our focus on Jesus Christ allows us to set aside what we cannot know in order to feel the presence of God with us. Some time ago I met Dr. Emilio Castro, General Secretary of the World Council of Churches. Rather than ask him about his work, I presumed that the need to understand grief theologically was more important. "How," I asked him, "do you as a pastor deal with death, particularly the death of a child?"

Dr. Castro was gracious in his response. "I have no answers. I hope that the family I go to visit is not home, that they will not open their door to me. If they are home and let me in, I sit and listen, as they talk about how they feel."

That evening, I told this story to bereaved parents. They didn't care who Dr. Castro was, but when they heard what he had said, there was a flood of agreement. "Yes," they said, almost as a group. "Being there is the only help."

In their suffering, bereaved parents have learned that having someone there is the helping gesture they need. They have also come to reject any answers that do not include the accompaniment of others.

Similarly, those who were with Jesus in the garden of Gethsemane did not know what to say to him. Once again, in Mark 14:36, Jesus acknowledges that God is all-powerful and all-loving, saying, "Abba, Father, for you all things are possible; remove this cup from me; yet not what I want, but what you want."

Theologian Dorothee Soelle comments on this part of the life of Jesus Christ in her book *Suffering,* where she looks at the Gethsemane experience. She writes (pp. 79, 81):

> Thus Jesus prayed that he would be spared the agony that lay before him. But to this plea he receives no answer. God is silent, as he has been so often in the history of mankind, and Jesus remains alone with his repeated cry, his fear of death, his insane hope, his threatened life. . . . In Gethsemane, Jesus made two futile attempts: he implored his father to spare him, and he asked people to console him. . . . Precisely that makes him one with all people and their indifferent neighbors.

Jesus' life and humanity are not a sugar-coated earthly version of heaven. Without going into a long description of Jesus' life as we know it from scripture, we can accept Soelle's summary, that it was "one with all people and their indifferent neighbors." Everyone suffers, perhaps not as a bereaved parent, but everyone suffers. We are all indifferent in one way or another to the suffering of our neighbors.

If we accept this interpretation of the life of Jesus, and create our expectations from it, do our expectations not in fact coincide with our experience?

Aren't bereaved parents alone? Don't they cry out, "Remove this loss from me?" Do not their friends fall asleep at the kitchen table? Isn't their life one with the life and humanity of Jesus Christ?

Where is the hope? Why shouldn't we be angry with God? Where is some sign that God understands? If now our experience coincides with our expectations, is God both all-powerful *and* all-loving? Where is the hope we have been promised?

Once again we read scripture to see what Jesus says about the tragedy that besets us all. Jesus' words are quoted in Matthew 5:43–45.

> You have heard that it was said, "You shall love
> your neighbor and hate your enemy." But I say to you,
> Love your enemies and pray for those who persecute you,
> so that you may be children of your Father in heaven; for
> he makes his sun rise on the evil and on the good, and
> sends rain on the righteous and on the unrighteous.

Jesus did not ignore the suffering of others but called all people to love both neighbor and enemy. Compassion, like the sun, shines on the evildoers and on the good. Suffering, like rain, falls on the just and the unjust. Jesus is one with all people who suffer, because God sends sun and rain on Jesus and on all people. Just as they came to Peter, James, and John and the others in Gethsemane, sun and rain come to every person.

Hope arises when we realize that our suffering makes us one with the life and humanity of Jesus. Hope does not bring back our child. We still get angry, even angry with God. But as we are one in Jesus' life, we find understanding. We realize that although God is silent when we cry out in anger, God is present with us as well. God understands that being there is the only help. In that we find hope.

10 EXPERIENCE THE PRESENCE OF GOD

At first, the pain parents feel when their child dies is so intense that shock functions to protect them. The full grief of the loss is not experienced all at once. But as the shock wears off, the pain increases and they seem to get worse rather than better.

Unless people have had this same experience, they really don't understand why the bereaved parent doesn't begin to recover. They don't understand that grief has driven the parent into a state of isolation from the rest of the world. Even the rest of the family ceases to exist as the parent is isolated by grief.

When Marlys was killed, Fran went into shock, just to survive. She was unaware of anyone around her and has little memory of the first few days. She didn't even realize how alone she was. As the full impact began to break through into her consciousness—that Marlys would never be with her again in this life, and they would no longer be able to talk together—Fran realized she really was alone with her grief. Even her other children didn't know how alone she was.

Lynn, Fran's younger daughter, who was then sixteen years old, was frightened too. Before all the family gathered, during the first few hours after Marlys was taken to the hospital, Lynn stayed at the home of a friend. When we talked to her on the phone, before Marlys had been brought down from surgery, Lynn said she didn't want to come to the hospital. Although I had no authority to do so, I told her she could bring a friend if she wanted, but she had to come. Fran, Lynn, and Lynn's good friend ended up staying in a nearby hotel until other arrangements were made.

In her inexperience or in simple fear of what was going on—probably both—Lynn wanted to make the impact of the tragedy less, so she wanted to stay away. As you can see from the poem she wrote, in the dedication to this book, Lynn needed to be there at the hospital to see her sister, to know firsthand what will forever be with her in memory. She needed to know what had permanently changed her life, her mother's life, her brother's life, and the lives of other relatives.

My fifteen-year-old son, John, gave Lynn a hunting knife that she carried with her for the next few days for protection, even in school. She didn't know if someone would be after her too. No one then or now knows why Marlys was murdered or who did it. How could Lynn not be afraid? Both she and John laugh about the knife now. But at that time these young people were reacting to their fear, fear that was real and justified. Of course, Fran noticed none of this, only later learning of the knife.

After the funeral, Fran and Lynn moved from the hotel to the home of a friend from church. They could not go back to the house where Marlys had been murdered. The murder had not been solved, and so what had been their home was now a place of danger for them. (It still remains a place of horror, as the memory of finding Marlys will always be with Fran.)

Lynn finished the few days left in her school year, and Fran, in shock, stayed hidden with friends. The first weeks were very painful. The investigation was not leading to an arrest. Suspicions were high. The police talked to everyone even remotely connected to Marlys and the family.

At that time, Fran has said, she felt totally alone, even among the family and friends who were near. It was as though everyone had been taken from her. Only much later did she realize how alone she felt. She felt like Job, whose story is told in the Bible.

As sad as it is to say, when Fran noticed how alone she was, the pain got worse. People were with her, and still others wanted to be with her and help her, but the pain was hers alone, so she was all alone.

Or was she? If the theology of accompaniment has value, Fran was not alone; others were with her. If the theology of accompaniment is really a working theology, thus offering understanding of God's action in our lives, Fran should have noticed. At least, Fran was not as alone as Job. Not only was Job set upon by disease and personal pain, all his children were taken from him.

In the first two chapters of Job, Satan is given permission by God to test Job, almost as if in a wager that a faithful servant will endure everything and remain faithful. In Job 1:12, we read, "The LORD said to Satan, 'Very well, all that he has is in your power; only do not stretch out your hand against him!' So Satan went out from the presence of the LORD." As part of the test, Job's seven sons and three daughters are killed.

This book of the Bible is one of the hardest to read. For bereaved parents it is especially difficult. Suffering is heaped on a blameless man, and even his children are taken from him. A first reaction to this from grieving parents is that God has some-how punished Job, and them, by taking away their children. Doesn't the Lord say "all that [Job] has is in your power," and doesn't Satan take these lives without hesitation?

Is there truth here for the parent whose young son is killed by a drunken driver? Is God testing a parent when leukemia takes a beautiful daughter in her teens? Was Fran's faith at stake when Marlys was murdered?

These are serious questions for people of faith. We cannot answer them by ignoring this part of the Bible. Rather, we can find answers where the promises of scripture merge with our experiences. In that merger we find understanding, and when we understand, we can give help to others. We ask, "What is said for today, for us?"

So what conclusion can we draw from the book of Job? Is it that tragedy which comes into our lives, especially when it is unexpected or undeserved in our view, is allowed to happen because God wants to test us?

Fran and I would say that the answer to this question is *no*! This is not the expectation we should take from the Bible, not the expectation we should live with. Rather, we believe that scripture tells us Job's own expectation was that God would treat him fairly.

Job was blameless, at least as much as any human being can be free from blame. The tragedy that befell him was not the direct result of any personal action or inaction. Job did not understand the source of his misfortune. He was first made into a bereaved parent, as his ten children were taken from him in a violent death. Then he was inflicted with painful illnesses, which drove him to wish he had not been born. His wife and his extended family and his friends were of no comfort. In fact, almost everyone who comments on this book points out how his three friends don't understand. But Job persisted in his expectation that God somehow understood, even when his friends and even Job himself did not. Eventually, Job met God and had an opportunity to test this belief with experience.

Job may have been blameless, and we may not be. Job suffers a great loss: ten children dying a senseless death. We are afflicted by grief when one of our children dies. We know a few parents who have had several children die, and no, we do not truly understand their grief. But Job is shown to us as having less blame and more sorrow than most, if not all, have had to bear. Out of his story we can derive certain expectations.

Primary among these is the expectation that we will have our answers from God when we ourselves are standing before God. Before that happens, we do not expect to be given understanding, and others, certainly, will not understand what we feel. Our expectation is that we will notice that we are alone, and we will seek answers from God.

One fantasy that many grieving parents have is to imagine that they are able to stand before God and ask, or more often demand, that God tell them why their child died. The question is not asked from an intellectual perspective—why did the medical treatment fail, or why did my child have to be on that street or in that car at that time? Rather, the question is accusative— "How could you let this happen to my child?"

This is a fantasy question, and we really know the answer— rain falls alike on the just and the unjust, and there is injustice and misery in the world. Our child had bad luck. Even when children have taken their own lives, in suicide or reckless self-destructive conduct, it is really just bad luck, isn't it?

Our child is dead. Although we may know and even comprehend the medical reasons and the circumstances of what happened at that specific place and time, we can't discount the value of our child's life and say that it was just bad luck. Luck takes the meaning out of that life and reduces all life to random happenings.

If we continue the fantasy, we ask God why this life ended at this time in this way. What, we ask of God, was your doing in this? If it is just luck, just bad luck for our child and random good luck for the neighboring child, then our lives and our belief in God have no meaning. We would not even bother God for an answer.

Eventually, Job is allowed to ask his questions of God. Before then, Job is in dialogue with his three friends, and all the answers are tried and fail. Job points to sinners and wicked ones who have a great life, living in glory and wealth to an old age. Moreover, these wicked persons do not suffer the loss of their children. Job sees that the sins of the father do not always visit the sons. Finally, after thirty-seven chapters, Job has his chance to stand before the Lord.

But Job's opportunity to question God evaporates in the whirlwind from which God speaks. God asks the questions and demands that Job tell him if Job can create universes and defeat monsters and do all wondrous things. Job admits he cannot.

But is the gloriousness of God and the frailty and failure of humans the only message? Job speaks to God (42:2–6):

> I know that you can do all things, and that no purpose of yours can be thwarted. "Who is this that hides counsel without knowledge?" Therefore I have uttered what I did not understand, things too wonderful for me, which I did not know. "Hear, and I will speak; I will question you, and you declare to me." I had heard of you by the hearing of the ear, but now my eye sees you; therefore I despise myself, and repent in dust and ashes.

Is that all? Perhaps if Fran were more like Job she would be able to stand before God and be humbled, and God would restore her daughter. Chapter 42 ends with Job again having seven sons and three daughters. He dies an old man, after seeing his sons and his sons' sons, three generations.

When Fran faces God, in this life or at the end of her days, it is not unreasonable to expect that she might understand a

God who can create universes and defeat monsters and do all wondrous things, as Job finally understood. When Fran faces God, she too might give up her questions, no longer demanding to know why Marlys was murdered. After all, Marlys will already have had her chance to understand and perhaps ask the same questions. Marlys has already stood before God.

The expectation that we get from reading the book of Job is that only when we meet God will we achieve that understanding and only then will we not need to ask questions. We will not need to know why the child we love so much has been taken from us. We will not be concerned with luck. Meeting God will be enough. Job's experience with God merged with his legitimate expectations, and Job understood. We too can expect understanding when we experience the presence of God.

The question that remains is this: Do we have to wait until our life as we know it on earth has ended before we experience the presence of God? Is there anything in the book of Job that will give us the legitimate expectation that we can experience this presence of God now, here in our grief? Is there anything in scripture that will give us this answer? May we have understanding now, before some future time and place in which we may believe but about which we know nothing?

Once again we turn to the book of Job. In Job's worst misery, as he feels so abandoned, as he notices that he is in fact alone, he makes this observation: "From the city the dying groan, and the throat of the wounded cries for help; yet God pays no attention to their prayer" (Job 24:12).

Job's expectation is that God will answer his prayers. Job's experience is that such an answer, and such an understanding, does not come until one is in the presence of God. What can be our experience? If Job says that God pays no attention to the prayers of those whose souls cry for help, to whom do we look for help?

The answer is that those who have been wounded and have somehow survived are called on to respond to those who are crying out now. We look not to ourselves but to our fellow sufferers.

The answer is that we must be there for the newly bereaved, because in being there we meet God. Only when we recognize the ministry of accompaniment will we too see God and have understanding in this life, as Job did. God sent his son, Jesus Christ. We must seek Jesus in those who also need him.

11 START THE HEALING
BY HELPING OTHERS

A fifty-eight-year-old lawyer friend of ours died after a struggle with cancer. He was survived by his wife, his brother, and other family members. He was also survived by his mother.

When I spoke with the mother, I introduced myself and said that I understood her pain. She just looked at me. Then I said, "We lost our daughter when she was eighteen." She started to cry and said, "Then you do understand. It hurts so much. I am trying to be brave, for his brother." I held her hand and told her, "I know how it hurts. It will take time. It will take a long time, but others have endured. You will also." She didn't believe me, but she thanked me.

Fran is the first to say that our friend's mother was right. She will never really recover from the loss of her child, even a fifty-eight-year-old son. But if people acknowledge her pain, and if those who have been there show her, by being there, that they survived, she will have a chance to heal.

The healing that is necessary if a parent is ever to be able to function after the death of a child does take a long time. It is a recovery in a sense, because we do function in society again. It is a recovery also because the scars are always with us, as when surgical amputation helps us to overcome a disease.

We are never the same but, within the limits of the surgery, we are able to function.

The analogy of surgery is very helpful. We need a skilled surgeon to perform the operation. This is like the comfort and care that other bereaved parents can give. When someone who has been in grief and appears to have survived, if not recovered, sits with the newly grieving and offers comfort, their recovery can begin and the other person's can continue.

But we also need nurses and nurses' aides, and the other support staff of a hospital, in order to recover. These are the friends and relatives, who are perhaps not really aware of the parent's pain but still offer comfort. Someone has to put that cup of tea by your side just when it is needed.

More than ten years after Marlys was murdered, we were relaxing in our living room after dinner with a friend. This friend was a fairly recent acquaintance and did not know much about us. During the conversation, as we exchanged stories about our pasts, we started to talk about Marlys's murder. Our friend was interested.

As we talked, we began to tell the story once again, and many memories came back. We were reciting our history, our memory of some event. One of us would say something and the other made additions or corrections. Then one of us talked about events and the other would fill in the details. We felt affirmed that the tragedy of Marlys's murder could again be told and we both could express our feelings.

All through the telling, we made our separate roles clear. Fran's grief was primary, but the rest of us—Fran's other children and my children and me—all had grief and confusion and pain and rejection to deal with as well.

What was interesting about this evening of friendship was that our friend was in the middle of difficult times, and we had invited him over to be of comfort to him. We reached out with no thought of our own needs. Yet in our attempt to offer comfort, we were comforted. Our new friend showed compassion and admitted that he didn't know how Fran could have survived Marlys's death. Fran's reply was simple. "I really didn't start healing until I started helping others."

We have made a distinction between recovery and healing. To recover from the death of a child to the point where we once again can function in society is just one step in the continuing life of those left behind by such a death. It is essential to be able to function, although tragically some people never even reach this state.

To go beyond mere functioning, to once again have meaning in your life, is to experience healing. Helping others is more than functioning and can become a very positive experience. Helping others can give important meaning to the life that was lost as well as to the lives of those who continue.

Recovery allows one to function in society. Healing allows others to function better. The difference between recovery and healing is the difference between being able to say "I made it through another day" and "I feel good about helping someone today." Over and over we have said that the grief from the loss of a child is great. We are in great pain, so much that we can't function. We can't go to work, and we can't cook a meal.

In time, particularly with the help of others who have been there, we can go to work and cook a meal. The meal even tastes good. But the pain is still with us. We are still looking inward in our grief. Eventually, someone who is in pain comes to our attention, and we reach out to help, even by a small gesture. Our pain, even for a moment, is less than what we know the other person is experiencing. We begin to see that our pain is less important than the pain of others, and we let them know that. We start to heal at that time.

Grief is pain that one cannot physically touch. It is a pain where there is emptiness. Think about my earlier analogy, comparing the death of a loved one to an amputation. The arm is gone, and we know it, even though we may not consciously think about it every minute of the day. But it is still gone. We can control the rest of our body, and we can learn to live a relatively normal life without that arm. Yet we know we will never be the way we were before our loss. We are different now. Others may forget. Some people expect us to get on with life. They know that it has been several months now, or perhaps several years, and they see us eating just fine with the other hand. They assume everything is good. They may even say to us, "Gee, you don't look like you've lost a child." Inside, we are in pain, missing this child we used to be able to reach out and touch. We want to hug our child, be with our child. But how can we hug with a missing arm?

12 WHERE DO WE GO FOR HEALING?

To continue the medical analogy, as we seek to understand the absence of our child in our lives, we should ask a question: Where is the hospital? Where do we go for healing?

Ideally, this place of healing would be the church. That is what a church is for, isn't it? Unfortunately, the church does not always function as a place of healing. Unfortunately, there are people in the church who are uncomfortable with those in pain. It is sad to say, but many of those parents who have lost a child to death no longer attend church, even if they have recovered and are functioning in other parts of their lives. They stay away, even when they are healing and helping others in their grief. Why is the church not a place of healing?

This problem, seeking to understand what the church is and what its proper role is, is as old as the church itself. There are many illustrations we could select, in scripture and in writings of the many churches in the world, as we try to find answers. One example is an event described in Mark 2:15–17, where Jesus is questioned about his table fellowship.

> And as he sat at dinner in Levi's house, many tax collectors and sinners were also sitting with Jesus and his disciples—for there were many who followed him.
> When the scribes of the Pharisees saw that he was eating

with sinners and tax collectors, they said to his disciples,
"Why does he eat with tax collectors and sinners?"
When Jesus heard this, he said to them, "Those who are
well have no need of a physician, but those who are sick;
I have come to call not the righteous but sinners."

Simply stated, this text from the Bible demonstrates that the church leaders, the Pharisees, did not understand why Jesus spent time with those outside the established religious community. Many religious leaders see this text as a call to evangelize, to seek out the ones outside the church, to convert nonbelievers. They call on sinners to repent, and they develop programs to reach the unsaved.

The religious community is full of good intentions, striving to bring new members into their congregations. Yet people in grief leave the churches, and we cannot avoid asking why. Why do those who are in pain attend less often, and still less often, until they no longer attend at all? The same religious leaders who feel the need to evangelize do not even think that sinners whom Jesus came to call could be inside the church, needing a physician because they are also sick.

What good is it to join a church, we ask, if the newly converted find no comfort there once they are members? What good is it to be a lifelong member of a church if we find no comfort in the church when we are in grief? When we need help, and when there is not even a basic understanding of our need for help, we too will be outside the church.

The sinners referred to in Mark 2:15–17 are outside the church, unclean, not part of the community. If church leaders do not recognize themselves in this text, do not see themselves acting in the same way as the Pharisees, how can we expect them to minister to us in our outsideness?

We know we hurt, and we know there are no easy answers.

Is it that the religious leaders cannot sit with us, day after day, week after week, year after year, as we express our pain in ways that are often hurtful, if not just plain boring, to those who do not feel the pain? Our grief places us outside the church, even when we're in the church building.

Many clergy people have not felt the pain and anguish of the loss of a child. Does that mean they cannot understand? Too often the answer is yes. And because they don't know what to do, and because they themselves don't know how to find a physician, they give up or ignore the bereaved parents who need help.

Often no one—not the pastor or priest, not the elders, deacons, or lay leaders—know how to deal with those bereaved church members who no longer function as they did before their child died. After all, they seem to think, if loving Jesus is supposed to bring joy to one's life, why are these people sitting in a back pew, all alone and crying? Are these grieving persons just an embarrassment to the church?

One Protestant pastor we know lost his daughter to cancer and two weeks later broke down in the pulpit as he attempted to preach a sermon. Soon after, the church leaders made him resign. They could not understand a pastor who was not comforted, somehow healed, because he was a pastor. He was an embarrassment to them.

Our pastor friend understands now how he had become an embarrassment. He knows there are no easy answers. He knows that a pastor who cannot handle grief is a threat to church members who have it all figured out and who have never had that struggle in their own lives. He is still a pastor, actually a much better pastor. When he sees someone grieving, in a pew or in a coffee shop, he takes time to be with them. He knows the physician. He knows where the hospital is. Of course! He has been there himself.

There are other exceptions as well. Some churches and pastors and priests do function well at reaching out to the wounded, hurting people of the world. Often these churches have bereaved parents in their leadership community. That is the best resource, to have access to one who has been outside seeking comfort and who has found it and brought it along.

But there are others who have found ways to reach out. The most effective way to help those in grief situations is, as I have stressed, to be there, to sit, to listen, to lend a shoulder. Just as in the passage quoted from Mark, the tax collectors and sinners and grieving parents, along with the alcoholics and cocaine addicts and divorced or abused or neglected persons, are in need of a physician.

Help comes as they sit together, and as the ones who have begun to recover reach out to help those who are less able to cope with their pain. Hurting people really don't start to heal until they start helping others.

People who hurt in the way that bereaved parents do have found that what they have been expecting from life and from God does not coincide with their bereavement experience. Yet when we reach out and begin helping others, we begin to understand that what we are experiencing in our grief is normal and valid. These experiences can be trusted. When we reach out and begin to help others, we see that God too has been reaching out. We find as we begin helping others that God is there with us in the helping.

Then hope arises, as for the first time we experience comfort from God, from scripture, from our faith. Let us look for that place of healing where we might find God.

Fran and I have said that our healing did not begin until we started helping others. When we do this, when we lend our shoulder to another who is in greater pain, we begin to surrender our own pain in the pain of the other. We are beginning to recognize the ministry of accompaniment. When we accompany those who are in pain, who do not even have what *we* have, we have begun to find God.

Remember Philippians 2:8 from Paul's letter to the church at Philippi: "And being found in human form, he humbled himself and became obedient to the point of death—even death on a cross."

If you expect to find God in the glorious places of this world, you will be disappointed. God is not experienced in all God's glory, with trumpets and angels and all wonderful things, not that way in this world. Just as we found in the last chapter as we began to understand the life and struggle that Job endured, we will not find our answers in gold and buildings and splendor.

In this world, if we would seek God, if we have expectations of comfort, the merging of our expectation and experience will be found in the life and humanity of Jesus Christ. As Jesus forgot his God self and became human, and in human form suffered death, we too must forget our self and reach out to help others. When we are willing to help others no matter what the cost, we will meet God; nowhere else.

13 WHERE IS GOD IN THIS?

The person who murdered Marlys on that eighth day of May in 1979 is still free. We don't know who the person is. We live with that lack of knowledge all the time. We don't know why Marlys was murdered. That is yet more knowledge we live without.

Marlys was murdered in the house where she lived, in the beautiful St. Croix Valley in Afton, Minnesota. She was buried in a cemetery that is part of Memorial Lutheran Church in Afton.

Many people contributed to a reward fund, which was to be used to encourage persons who had information about the murder to come forward. No one did. The police in charge of the investigation did as much as they could to find the person who killed Marlys. No one was arrested.

Money from memorial gifts and reward money was used to buy carillon chimes for Memorial Lutheran Church. The carillon bells ring out every day, loud and clear, over the valley of the St. Croix River. The bells sing out for everyone to hear.

Our hope is that the person who committed the murder can hear those bells every day. Our hope is that the person is reminded every day that those bells ring in Afton, Minnesota, because he or she took the life of another.

Our hope is that someday the murderer will be compelled to repent, and confess.

We don't hear the carillon bells any longer because we moved from Minnesota to the East Coast. But we often take comfort in knowing that the bells ring every day as a memorial to Marlys and others, as a reminder to her friends who miss her, and as a conscience in the peaceful St. Croix Valley.

The guilt the murderer feels is hard for us to know. We don't know if the person was on drugs and thus doesn't remember the crime, except for some vague understanding that some bad thing may have been done. We don't know if the person has a constant memory of the act of killing a human being and is tormented by a conscience. We don't even know whether the murderer is a man or woman.

One discussion we have had, together and with friends and family, centers on trying to understand how anyone could have killed Marlys. We don't know how one person could take another person's life under any circumstances. We certainly don't know how one human being can kill another. It doesn't make sense, even after sixteen years. To think of standing in the shoes of the murderer is too painful. We can't do it. We will never know what it is like to kill someone. In the specific, we ask how anyone can take the life of an eighteen-year-old girl who had no enemies that we know of, no sins hidden from us, no acquaintances who could be that evil. Was it a random event, an accident, or a mistake? Was Marlys even the intended victim?

Our discussion leads to philosophy and, almost always, to theology. Eventually, we conclude that the person who actually struck the blows committed an irrational act. Normal human beings aren't capable of such violence unless provoked or in the heat of combat.

We will never be able to understand Marlys's death, even if someone confesses. We will never be able to understand an act that makes no sense. It is not possible to put ourselves inside the mind of someone who does all that damage to another human being.

In a way, solving the murder will not make any difference because we still won't understand how someone could commit such an act. We ask ourselves how carillon chimes will bring such a person to pangs of conscience. We don't even know if it can. We can't understand what affects a conscience when we can't understand what causes such an irrational act.

In the same way, parents of children who die from automobile accidents, drowning, plane crashes, suicide, drug overdose, cancer, and similar causes will never understand how such a tragedy could happen. The death of a child happens by some random event, an accident, a twist of fate. Those things don't have a conscience either.

We are no different from any other bereaved parents. Fran's daughter has been taken from her, and no one has answered for the crime. Even if someone confessed tomorrow and told us why it happened, we could not really understand. The death of children from AIDS, or starvation, or disease, or poverty, or military exercises, or any other way is a mistake. None of us will understand why—at least not in this life.

More than that, what we have in common with others is that we are no more able to understand how God could let this death happen than other parents can understand such a fact. Even the one who killed Marlys had parents. We know that person's parents would feel terrible if they knew their child had killed someone. We also know that these parents would not understand why.

Both our conversations with each other and with friends and family, and theological issues have led us to look at events from a different perspective. Instead of asking how God could let our child die, and instead of asking how God could let any child die, we ask a different question: Where is God in this?

We don't hold God responsible for Marlys's murder. God didn't use the blunt instrument and strike her down. God doesn't directly cause the death of any child. We don't ask why God causes the deaths of children. Rather than ask why, we ask: "Where is God in this?"

We know that individual human beings cause the death of others. We know that natural events, like earthquakes and hurricanes, cause death. We know that disease and poverty and oppression cause death. Social conditions can cause the death of children, in Somalia and Guatemala and the ghettos of large American cities. We do not know that God causes death.

Perhaps the carillon bells ring for our conscience, as a reminder that there is much we can do to help others who are in greater need than we are. There are so many causes of death, and so few sources of life. The memorials, the carillon bells, are a reason to do good.

14 MEMORIALS GIVE US HOPE

It is easy to find examples in the Bible of death and destruction. Sometimes there is justice, and sometimes those who die are innocent. When an entire group of people is killed, as one can read in the Bible, particularly the Old Testament, it appears that God has caused these deaths. Where is God in these events and in the lives of those left behind?

A review of every instance in the Bible is beyond the scope of this book. However, it is important that each bereaved parent— and everyone else, for that matter—look at the issue of God's role in these stories of death. When you go to the Bible, for comfort or for understanding or for whatever reason, you should look at the stories and teachings seriously. It is important to ask the right questions, particularly for bereaved parents but also for everyone else. Let us look at one example.

The book of Judges describes Sisera, one of the most evil people in all of human recollection. He killed many innocent people. Judges 4 starts by telling us that the Lord sold the people of Israel into the hand of Jabin, the king of Canaan, because they had done evil in the sight of the Lord. Sisera was the commander of the army, and he oppressed the people of Israel cruelly for twenty years (Judges 4:3).

Deborah, a prophetess and judge of Israel, tells Barak, who has an army of liberation, that "the LORD will sell Sisera into the hand of a woman" (Judges 4:9). This certainly seems to say that God has a role in these events.

Sisera goes to the tent of Jael, the wife of Heber, one who was at peace with Sisera's king. Jael offers him rest in her tent, and Sisera accepts. As the chapter ends, Sisera tells Jael, "'Stand at the entrance of the tent, and if anybody comes and asks you, "Is anyone here?" say, 'No'" (Judges 4:20). Then we learn that "Jael took a tent peg, and took a hammer in her hand, and . . . drove the peg into [Sisera's] temple, until it went down into the ground." So Sisera died.

Jael then finds Barak, who is pursuing Sisera, and takes him to her tent to find Sisera dead. The story ends with the words, "So on that day God subdued King Jabin of Canaan before the Israelites" (Judges 4:23).

The next chapter, Judges 5, is the Song of Deborah, which is a poetic reflection on her role as a judge and prophetess. Beginning at verse 24, Deborah's song tells the story of Sisera's death at the hand of Jael:

> Most blessed of women be Jael, the wife of Heber
> the Kenite, of tent-dwelling women most blessed. He
> asked water and she gave him milk, she brought him curds
> in a lordly bowl. She put her hand to the tent peg and her
> right hand to the workmen's mallet; she struck Sisera a
> blow, she crushed his head, she shattered and pierced his
> temple. He sank, he fell, he lay still at her feet; at her feet
> he sank, he fell; where he sank, there he fell dead.

But do not overlook verse 28:

> Out of the window she peered, the mother of Sisera
> gazed through the lattice: "Why is his chariot so long in
> coming? Why tarry the hoofbeats of his chariots?"

Note that Sisera's mother's anguish is recorded in the Song

of Deborah. Is it a memorial to an evil man? We don't think so. But it might be a memorial to the grief all parents have when their own child dies and the parents are left to grieve.

We don't suggest that Sisera's death wasn't justified, especially in a time in history when violent death was expected. We don't suggest that Jael is any less blessed in Israel's history, for she clearly helped save many lives with her act. Deborah did the right thing, we think, in praising Jael. But she also did the right thing when she recorded a memorial to the grief of Sisera's mother.

The Bible speaks to the recognition of grief and to the presence of God in that grief. Both biblical and present-day events show us that God is active in human lives. Our need now is to understand that God is with us, and with everyone, in their grief.

To us, the memorial carillon bells do not toll forgiveness over the St. Croix River valley in Afton, Minnesota. We hope that the one who killed Marlys hears those bells and is brought to repent. We also hope that that person's mother and father, if either are alive and in the valley, also know that God will be with them when their time comes. The message they send, we believe, is that God, through the church but also without the consenting knowledge of the church, is with us all in our grief.

Memorials are a fine thing and should be erected, with dignity, for the memory of the child who has gone on before us. But memorials are not the answer. Memorials, even as great as the pyramids in Egypt, are no substitute for the child who has died. Marlys is worth more to Fran than all the bells in the world, now and ever.

But at least with a memorial we are looking out at the world rather than in at our grief. We are hoping someone will notice. We are like Sisera's mother, standing at the window, looking for our child, hoping where there is no hope.

Memorials give us hope by helping us to look out at the world, but we need something beyond memorials if we are to go beyond our grief. We will never forget our child, but we do no good to that child's memory if our grief destroys us and we are not somehow able to help others.

Again the Bible can help. This time we are not looking for a story but for clarification. What is the hope that we would get? Listen to these words from Romans 8:24–25: "For in hope we were saved. Now hope that is seen is not hope. For who hopes for what is seen? But if we hope for what we do not see, we wait for it with patience." Certainly this is true for bereaved parents. Our hope is that our child is with God. That is what prevents us from total despair. Our child has now seen the majesty of God, like Job, and all is well for Marlys.

What we hope for we cannot see. If we hope that memorials will heal our grief, we are hoping for something we cannot see. If the memorials help us to turn outward, from ourselves and our grief, toward others, then our hope really is that God is with us. And while we cannot see God, not directly and face to face, we hope.

We hope God is with the one who set in motion the mistake that killed Marlys. We hope God is speaking, louder than the carillon bells, calling the killer to repentance. We are able to get anger out and to take vengeance, however briefly, by having bells ring in the ears of Marlys's murderer. We are hoping— guessing, really—that we have done something.

The memorial gave us hope that justice would be done, that the truth would come out, and that we could do something to punish the one who killed her. This isn't a pure motive. It isn't what Christ would do. But just as God lets us know that Sisera's mother waits and mourns, God is with the one who hears the carillon bells in that tiny Minnesota town. Maybe that person will repent.

There are other kinds of memorials that do good and that are used by bereaved parents as necessary and legitimate outlets for the anger, hurt, and despair they suffer. Memorials tell the story that we have been deprived of our child and we hurt. We want others to know it, and because we want to recover in some way from the intense pain we feel, we want to do some good.

Money is given as a memorial, for cancer research or hospice programs, or rescue equipment. Bereaved parents work to stop others from driving drunk, to change safety laws on college campuses, or to have dangerous products removed from the market. Stained glass windows provide beauty in a church. Other equally precious gifts are given, sometimes anonymously but always with the hope that we are keeping alive the memory of one whom we miss greatly and that others will remember our child too.

If we didn't have memorials, we wouldn't have anything to say. We would have no hope, even in things we can see or hear or touch. But we do have hope. We have reached out to tell the world of our pain, and we have started to heal. We will never recover, but we hope. We start to heal.

15 REACH OUT IN LOVE

Our goal as we seek to heal from the grief and pain of Marlys's death is not that we somehow fully recover. We don't expect to be happy and untroubled. We can't deny the value of her life and her personhood. Marlys's death means a great deal to us, and it always will, because her life meant so much. Now, in this life at least, all we have is our memory of her. That must be preserved.

In the first year after Marlys died, we both went to the cemetery at the little white church on the hill. Fran took pleasure in tending the grave, placing flowers and decorations, making it look nice. I stood and watched and lifted the heavy things. We knew her body was still in the casket, but we did not consider that Marlys had a presence at the cemetery.

In 1985, six years after Marlys was murdered and almost five years after we moved to Pennsylvania, we moved the casket and had a small graveside service with family and friends, because Fran wanted to continue tending the grave. It felt right to do, and we did it. It still feels right, in part because we are comfortable with having a place to visit, especially on holidays.

One holiday, however, led to a bad day during the eleventh Christmas after Marlys died. Fran had been planning on taking a wreath to Marlys's grave and needed some help clearing snow. I wanted to help choose it and had suggested stopping several times when it was not possible, so Fran bought it when I was at work, and that hurt my feelings. After dinner that day, the bad day got worse. Both of us had hurt feelings, and old pains came back for a little while.

We came to our senses, fortunately, because this had happened before, and we were able to go to the grave and place the wreath in just the right place. It looked nice, and at Christmas we went back and lit the candle we took from the candlelight church service we attended on Christmas Eve. We got through the bad day because we knew that feelings were sensitive, especially at holidays and anniversaries. After all, we had been having good and bad days for the last eleven years, and we understand, almost.

We will never recover from Marlys's murder, but we are healing. We have hope that has come from reaching out to tell the world of our pain. From that hope, we need to see progress, so that we can be reminded that we are healing.

We recently looked at a picture taken of us on the first Christmas after Marlys's death, as we posed by the tree. The best thing that can be said about the picture is that it shows just how far we have come. There is comfort in physical proof that healing takes place where others can see it. This is the experience bereaved parents have when they reach out to the newly bereaved. There is comfort in helping the newly bereaved, just by being there and saying we understand. As a mother reaches out to others, she sees herself as she was at first. Nobody wants to look that bad.

In that Christmas photo, Fran looks to be in great pain. She was, of course. Photos of Fran now don't show that pain; it is covered over with the scars of healing. The best pictures of Fran now are taken when she is helping others or is talking about her efforts to do this.

Fran's marriage to Marlys's father, Jim Wohlenhaus, ended fourteen years before Marlys's death in 1979. She has not had to deal directly with the very real issue of the relationship a bereaved parent has with his or her spouse during the early years of healing. Both Fran and Jim had other relationships in 1979, and both have continued on their separate paths, taken years earlier. After the funeral, each of them went back to those paths to seek comfort and healing in different ways. They had neither the advantages nor the disadvantages that belong to a couple who are together when a child of their marriage dies.

Often, however, parents suffer the pain and grief of the death of a child together, in the marriage that brought that child into the world. How can one spouse help the other recover when each one is in so much need of help? Although we have seen statistics that many parents of children who have died get a divorce, that has not been our experience. The divorce rate for bereaved couples whom we meet and know is lower than the divorce rate for other couples.

Of course, our experience is with bereaved couples who are helped and are helping others. The couples we know are couples who reach out, who find hope in memorials and in working with others. In their pain and grief, they have one advantage, and that is they understand what the other spouse is experiencing. If they hang on, not taking their anger out on each other, and if there is love for the other, they can survive together and have an even stronger marriage. The healing process is the same. Reaching out to another in pain and grief is absolutely essential for the healing of self. If you can reach out to your spouse—and many do—this is a great act of love.

The traditional biblical understanding of love between couples comes from chapter 13 of Paul's First Letter to the Corinthians. This is often read at marriage services and is known as the "love chapter." It is even more appropriate to read these words in an attempt to understand what is needed for a marriage to survive the death of a child. It is worthwhile reading all of 1 Corinthians 13, but verses 12 and 13 are particularly relevant.

> For now we see in a mirror, dimly, but then we will see face to face. Now I know only in part; then I will know fully, even as I have been fully known. And now faith, hope, and love abide, these three; and the greatest of these is love.

There is a great opportunity for couples who seek to survive together in this most horrible grief when their child dies, to reach out in love to the partner with whom they joined together in love to bring this child into the world. For most couples, this leads to healing for both partners. Those couples who are not successful in staying together after a child dies often say the marriage was bad anyway. We know that without a strong bond of love, there will not be enough reaching out by one for the other. When each dwells on private pain and grief, when they don't reach out to each other—when even one does not reach out to the other—the self comes first. There is no healing in that.

Perhaps they will find other partners who will love them and want to be loved by them. Perhaps it will have happened before the child dies, and perhaps it will happen after. In the new relationship, comfort and healing will come, if it does, when both partners reach out to love and comfort the other, rather than dwell on their own feelings.

Understanding will come in time if there is enough love. They will be glad if they can even see in a mirror dimly. The love chapter of First Corinthians will have special meaning for them as they seek to understand the grief and the hope that love can give for healing, scars and all.

16 LOVE IS THE ANSWER

In the photograph from our first Christmas after Marlys's death, I look both concerned and confused. I've tried for sixteen years to deal with my grief and Fran's grief, and most of the confusion is gone now. But the concern remains. I'll forget, and then all of a sudden I'm concerned because Fran is having a bad moment, perhaps remembering something.

Being there and listening, even when you hear the same things over and over, is very difficult, but it is absolutely essential in the first few years. Actually that job isn't ever over; it's always important to have a sensitive ear ready to listen to the pain come out. Eventually, it is even possible to draw out the pain, knowing when to ask about a bad day.

The stepparent has to remember that he or she has not experienced that mind-numbing grief which forces the mind to slam shut and let nothing penetrate the consciousness except the pain of the loss of the child. Stepparents must understand that for their spouse their love is not a substitute for a child and never will be.

The stepparent also has to understand something that is impossible to understand and at the same time repress his or her own feelings. It is especially hard to repress feelings of impatience and of being excluded. These are two of the hardest emotions to ignore.

It is easy to say that it is time your spouse was over this grief thing. Think it, then forgive yourself for not understanding and do something nice for your spouse. Never say it. It isn't true, in the first place, and it isn't your decision anyway.

It is also easy to claim some right to be included in the grief process. Stepparents have feelings too, and it is natural to want them recognized. Do that gently when the events relate to your life together, but don't ask to be part of the problem. Your spouse needs someone who will provide love until that time when he or she can give love in return. Be part of the solution, loving and putting the other ahead of yourself.

A stepparent will have grief as well, as one who knew the love of the child partly, perhaps, and who now can never have that love. I have said I wish Marlys were here to brighten my day. I'll never again have that experience with Marlys, anymore than Fran will. My loss gives me a small understanding of what Fran feels every day.

Even if a child has died before a stepparent came to know and love the grieving parent, some vital part of that mother or father is missing forever. The stepparent has lost the opportunity to experience things with the child that might have led to pleasant memories. Recognizing that will lead to an understanding of the pain held in the memories of the child's parent.

On bad days, a stepparent will feel left out, perhaps mistakenly, and will want to be part of something that he or she doesn't qualify to be part of. On our bad day just before our eleventh Christmas after Marlys died, we learned once again to share our feelings. After so many years, it is legitimate to talk about participation in memories. After so many years, it is a good day when we go to the cemetery together and light a candle. We both said that night that we have gone beyond cursing the darkness.

When stepparents really understand, we will try to be there for our spouse at the right time, ready to listen, as much as imperfect people can. We say this because the only way to fully love is to give oneself fully. Only when we give ourselves to another do we express our love in a meaningful way. Only when we forget our own needs and tend to the needs of others are we truly expressing love and not self-gratification. This is the message of Jesus we have found, to love as it is said in John 3:16–17. As you read these verses, try to keep in mind that God is a bereaved parent.

> For God so loved the world that he gave his only
> Son, so that everyone who believes in him may not perish
> but may have eternal life. Indeed, God did not send the
> Son into the world to condemn the world, but in order
> that the world might be saved through him.

It is hard to pick this Bible text up and insert it into the reality that is experienced by bereaved parents. Certainly no one would send a child to die for others. Even in wartime, the expectation is that our child will come home safely. Even if a child dies in an act of heroism, we wish someone else had been the hero, no matter how many others are saved. We can't think of loving anyone enough that we would give up our son or daughter for that person's sake. Then what does the text tell us?

We would give up our own lives if we could save the life of our child. Fran has said she truly wishes that she had died in Marlys's place, so Marlys could be alive. And Fran would trade her life for Marlys's if Marlys could be brought back to life today.

This is a common desire in bereaved parents. It is an expression of love for another—if not for all others—at least on a human scale. But on the human level we have no hope that our child will return, even in our place. Despite our love for our child, there is nothing in which we can place our faith that such a miracle would happen.

But if we have faith in God, we can have hope because such a miracle did happen. The miracle is the total self-denial of God in Jesus Christ, who suffered death on a cross. Christ who was God took on human form so that we all can have eternal life. This was done out of love. God expressed that love on a divine level when God sent his Son into the world, that the world would be saved and not condemned. God's gift of his Son is a gift of self that teaches us the meaning of life itself.

We have our faith, out of which comes hope, so that we might love, for in love is the answer. We would die that our child would live. Jesus Christ died that we all shall live. We need to understand, in a mirror dimly, perhaps, that God fully understands humanity in the life, death, and resurrection of Jesus Christ. What we know in part we will understand fully when we too stand before God.

17 CHRIST IS THE CHALLENGE

Our lives reflect our loss of Marlys, and our expressions of that loss include carillon bells and making visits to a cemetery, a monument of stone and a buried casket that Fran can tend. It isn't enough, but it is something. There is a peace that comes from having a place to go, both in this world and, we think, in the life to come.

Marlys's personality, her spirit, her soul is with God and will remain there until the end times. What those end times mean and what will happen then we do not understand. It is no more within our knowledge now than it was for Jesus or his closest disciples.

When Jesus was on the cross, one of the criminals there with him said, "Jesus, remember me when you come into your kingdom." And Jesus replied, "Truly I tell you, today you will be with me in Paradise" (Luke 23: 42–43).

Bereaved Christian parents all believe that their children are with Jesus now. We have no doubt that this is true. Fran and I will not be fully healed, however, until we are with Jesus and Marlys. That day is not this day.

What we know for sure is that if life as we know it is going to have any meaning, if reality is going to exist for us, that will happen as we keep the memory of our child alive. To make our life a reality in the face of our loss, Christ challenges us through helping others, so that the memory of our child never dies. Christ is the challenge.

We cannot just sit back and let ourselves die. No bereaved parent should do that. We want our child to live eternally. We have a desire to do something, to preserve our child's life in memory. The only way a child will live is through the work that we do, helping others. If we turn in on ourselves, we are not responding to that challenge of Christ.

What will we say, then, when we stand before God? The only time we will ever have Marlys back with us, to laugh and tease and play and work and love, will be when we stand before God in the end times. Marlys will be there with us, and we will have answers to those questions that we ask in vain now.

Our promise, which we take from the Bible, from God who entered into history, is that there will be judgment. We will stand before God, as Job did, and we will understand all. But that is then, and this is now. Now we have the life and the death and the resurrection of Jesus Christ. We are challenged to follow that life if we are to participate in it fully.

I have said earlier that Jesus Christ forgot his God self and became human and in human form suffered death on a cross. I also said that this means, at least in part, that we must be willing to die in order to have comfort in our pain. We must be willing to die for others, not for ourselves, for there is no obedience and humility in the latter.

We read earlier in Paul's Letter to the Philippians of the actions of Christ. Read what Paul has written (Phil. 3:8–11) about his own understanding of the challenge of Christ.

> More than that, I regard everything as loss because
> of the surpassing value of knowing Christ Jesus my Lord.
> For his sake I have suffered the loss of all things, and I
> regard them as rubbish, in order that I may gain Christ

and be found in him, not having a righteousness of my own that comes from the law, but one that comes through faith in Christ, the righteousness from God based on faith. I want to know Christ and the power of his resurrection and the sharing of his sufferings by becoming like him in his death, if somehow I may attain the resurrection from the dead.

We are all like Paul in wanting the resurrection from the dead. Not all of us are like Paul in wanting to become like Christ in his death, however, and this is the challenge we face. If we are to be like Christ, and like what Paul wants to be, we must accept the whole challenge. In order to share in the resurrection, Paul understands that he must share in Christ's suffering, becoming like him in his death.

If we do not have faith in the resurrection, all we have is this world at this time, with only the memory of our child. It is so sad when all one has is a memory. But if we do have faith in the resurrection, and in the challenge to live for others rather than ourselves, we have the hope that we too will become like Christ and Paul, and our child, and attain the resurrection from the dead.

Some people who read the Bible say that Jesus was abandoned by God while he was on the cross. Certainly Jesus' plaintive cry—"My God, my God, why have you forsaken me?" (Matt. 27:46; Mark 15:34)—leads one to think that the human Jesus at least felt alone.

But Luke reports (23:46) that Jesus said, "Father, into thy hands I commit my spirit." And John simply reports (19:30) that Jesus said, "It is finished" and then bowed his head and gave up his spirit.

We as Christians believe that Jesus was not only human but was and is also God, together with the Holy Spirit, in some way that we do not fully understand but have named the Trinity. And we as bereaved parents believe that God was not absent when Jesus died. God was silent but present, just as we are to be present for others who suffer in this world.

We have called the theology we present a theology of accompaniment. Being there for others, even being silent when there is nothing to say, is part of our theology. But there is more than mere presence; accompaniment means being willing to place others ahead of yourself when they are more in need of comfort.

Taken to its logical conclusion, accompaniment includes a willingness to die for others, that others may live. This is what Christ did, and this is what most parents would do for their children. We would die that our child could live, because we love our child. God took on human form and died on the cross that humanity might have eternal life, because God so loved the world.

This is how comfort from God coincides with the experience of living for God. This is the challenge of Christ.

Accepting the challenge of Christ is not simply a matter of saying something and being done with it. It is necessary to love another person enough to lay down your life. And we can't do that for our child. So we need to find a way to merge our expectation of being healed in Christ with an experience that makes the healing real for us. How does this happen?

One person whose story demonstrates a merger of expectation and experience is a doctor I met in the mountains of Nicaragua. This doctor, a native of Argentina who was educated in Europe, had been an atheist at one time in her life. Not long before I first met her, a nurse had been killed while giving vaccinations to children. Since no one else would go to continue the work, this doctor began to administer the vaccinations herself.

Walking with a thermos of vaccine over one shoulder and a rifle over the other, she seeks to bring health to those who have a great need for her help. She says she is no longer an atheist and has come to know what Jesus meant when he said, "They do not take my life from me, it is mine to give." This doctor has taken the words of Jesus (in John 10:17–18) and given them new meaning.

> For this reason the Father loves me, because I lay down my life, in order to take it up again. No one takes it from me, but I lay it down of my own accord. I have power to lay it down, and I have power to take it up again; I have received this command from my Father.

Her life could end soon as she walks in the face of danger, and yet she is turned toward God, facing God, with such clarity that she sees no contradiction between God's word and her own life. This is accompaniment.

Another story is more personal. Fran visited El Salvador as a tourist in 1978, the year before Marlys was murdered. She saw a beautiful countryside and beautiful people. She says quite honestly that she fell in love with El Salvador.

In March of 1987, Fran traveled again to El Salvador, this time to walk with the Mothers of the Disappeared as they commemorated the death of the martyred archbishop Oscar Romero, assassinated by a right-wing death squad in 1980 as he sought to end the violent civil war that was tearing his country apart. Fran went as part of an ecumenical group to celebrate Romero's death as a victory over the forces of evil. She went to participate in the delivery of a nation that she loves, El Salvador, a delivery by the hands of God.

Fran also went to deal with her own grief, in solidarity with those who would understand. She walked and prayed and worshiped with several hundred Mothers of the Disappeared. These mothers know the pain of loss when their children are taken from them, killed, and left to be found on body dumps. When they were in the basilica in San Salvador, praying to God for an end to the war, helicopters hovered above them, their rotors beating down on the church, beating with intimidation. When Fran came home, she admitted that during this worship service, at least, she would have put herself between the mothers and anyone intruding with a gun, to prevent arrests from being made.

Fran's testimony is very much like that of Paul, whom we paraphrase from the Second Letter to the Corinthians. In the hardships she underwent (in Minnesota or El Salvador) we should be quite certain that Fran was under extraordinary pressure. It was beyond her powers of endurance, so she gave up hope of surviving. But she did survive in her accompaniment. God was a comfort, not from a hidden place on high but from the understanding of those who had been comforted by the presence of those who understood.

Those moments of accompaniment do not last forever. Emotional solidarity with others who have somehow survived a very bad event is part of the process of forming scars. As we heal from our own tragedy and bereavement, we can help others. We can tell our own story. We can listen to the story of others. Most important, we can reach out to others in love.

The only way to oppose suffering is to be there and to accompany the ones who are suffering. We should read God's word, and we should pray. But we should take the time to sit in silence and acknowledge the grief and the loss. We should be there for those who do not understand why God has allowed this personal tragedy to occur and help them to find others who have survived.

As one is comforted, particularly by the presence of some-one who has already been there, hope arises out of the faith that God too is present. Hope becomes complete as the one who is suffering learns to help others more newly bereaved. There is a surrender of one's own pain in the pain of another.

As Jesus Christ says, "I give you a new commandment, that you love one another. Just as I have loved you, you also should love one another" (John 13:34).

If we accept the challenge of Christ, to love others as he has loved us, we will be healed. In this life we will give honor to the memory of our child, given in love. When finally we stand before God, we and our child will be fully healed in God's love.

Reach out in peace.